Confronting Toxic Othering

Understanding and Taming the Hydra

Introducing 'Critical Hydra Theory'

Thomas Arcaro, PhD

Praise for *Confronting Toxic Othering*

"Dr. Arcaro has offered us an amazing gift in our struggle to forge a more just future for all humans. This book presents a Hydra model representing the full range of privileging forces used to marginalize people across the globe. His concepts of 'toxic othering' and 'Critical Hydra Theory' are clear, compelling, and extraordinarily useful. These tools will help those who read this book to deepen their understanding of the root causes -and therefore pathways to solutions- of many of the social ills that we at the Centre for Peace and Justice address every day. This book is a must read for students and professionals alike."

> ***Manzoor Hasan OBE***
> Executive Director,
> Centre for Peace and Justice
> BRAC University, Bangladesh

"As a former humanitarian operations and policy practitioner, I believe this book not only explores some of the most challenging present-day questions facing the humanitarian response community but also offers incredible insights and new ways of thinking. It is a highly valuable text that will be an asset to those working on responses, developing policy, and conducting research."

> **Kirsten Gelsdorf, PhD**
> Professor of Practice of Leadership and Public Policy, Director of
> Global Humanitarian Policy,
> University of Virginia

"This book provides a unique perspective on global social issues. The image of the Hydra connects all the major privileging forces and helps the reader begin their own journey using critical Hydra theory to better understand the world around them. It is clear from the student comments throughout that the Hydra resonates with them and is a powerful metaphor for engaging critically with intersectionality and reflexively with privilege. I think it will be a great teaching tool. Prof Arcaro continues to lead pedagogical innovations."

> **Vaneeta D'Andrea, PhD**
> Professor Emerita
> University of the Arts London
> CEO World-wide Higher Education Consultancy

Confronting Toxic Othering

Prologue

We are all impacted by how others view us. Each human has various statuses, some of which we are born into like the color of our skin, and some of which we acquire or earn, for example, a university degree. Your master status in any situation is that part of you that is most important to those around you; it depends on the audience. In some situations, the fact that I present as a male is most salient, other times it is that I am from the Global North. Both are, in the majority of social situations, privileged status. But why is that so? What makes some statuses more valued than others?

Using the analogy of the mythical beast the Hydra, this book addresses the many privileging forces that impact all of us -every day- in each of our social interactions. The chapters in this book are edited versions of a series of blog posts that I wrote after attending an international gathering of humanitarian practitioners and researchers in Berlin, 2019. Many of the ideas discussed in this book were inspired by my students at Elon University and by the countless humanitarian workers that I have interviewed and become friends with over the last several years while researching and writing about the humanitarian sector.

The chapters are arranged in the order they were originally published, and this allows the reader to see the evolution of the idea over time. My blog writing has never been intended as a rigorous academic effort but more so a reflexive examination of the world through my lens as a sociologist. Work with the Hydra is ongoing, and more chapters will be added in the revised editions.

What are these privileging forces? They include patriarchy, racism, ableism, ageism, colonialism, paternalism, classism, heteronormativity, cisnormativity, and anthropocentrism, and all are 'baked into' our globalized world, perhaps most malignantly so in the Global North. Each is unique and powerful and can be examined separately, but their full impact is only fully understood by examining how each amplifies the others through the process of intersectionality. The premise of this book is that by understanding the body of the Hydra and what fuels its actions, we can begin to tame this beast.

This book offers a fresh perspective on the privileging forces that dominate our world. It will be useful for all humanitarians, students, and educators as they further their understanding of the many and persistent 'isms' that justify the systematic marginalization of others.

Acknowledgements

First, I want to acknowledge and give thanks to the staff at ALNAP for inviting me to their semi-annual meeting of academics studying the humanitarian sector and practitioners in this complex and critical sector. Being involved in the session on 'addressing privileging forces in the humanitarian sector' truly changed my view of the world.

I want to thank all my Introduction to Sociology, Sociological Theory, Sociology Through Film, and Global Social Problems students that have been in my classes since the fall of 2019 when the Hydra came to life. Student input has been critical over these last few years, and I owe much to the many bright minds that helped me expand and deepen my ideas about how the Hydra can be used to better understand privileging forces.

My Elon University research students Trevor Molin, Megan Hutchinson, and Erin Swisher had a major impact on this work. Their support and feedback have been both welcome and extraordinarily helpful.

Dr. Ahmed Fadaam deserves copious praise for his artwork on the Hydra and reminding me that taming, not defeating the Hydra is our ultimate goal.

Finally, and most importantly, I owe a debt of gratitude to the many humanitarian workers from all parts of the world that have shared their stories with me over the past 10 years.

Special thanks go to Linda Martindale for her helping edit this work. Without her patience and persistence, this project would not have happened. The final polishing and editing of this book were done by Maryanne Gicobi. Her care and vision have had a powerful impact on this project, and I owe her much.

8

Preface

In the fall of 2019 when I began writing this book George Floyd was alive and unknown and Covid-19 did not exist. So much has happened in the last two years. As I write this the US exit from Afghanistan is unfolding, the delta variant of Covid is stressing our health system to the max, and Rohingya are commemorating Genocide Remembrance Day. I had my students on the first day of class here at Elon consider what the world will look like when they are as old as me. One of them reckoned that it would be the year 2063. They then Googled predictions, based on the latest climate crisis news, concerning what the world would look like by then. That I feel some urgency addressing social justice in general and the climate crisis is a gross understatement. I hope this book can help in some small way to move us forward in addressing the myriad crises we face today.

We live in a world filled with increasingly complex social and environmental issues, gross economic inequalities, and all manner of situations where one group marginalizes, exploits, and even commits genocide on another. I believe there can be a different, more just world, and those who seek a better world need all possible available tools in this struggle. This book represents one modest tool which may be helpful to some as they try to make connections between the dizzying array of social justice issues not only at home but around the planet. My basic concept is not terribly new, and I certainly owe much to thinkers like bell hooks, Mahmood Mamdani, and Kimberlé Crenshaw and many others who saw interconnections between the various privileging forces long before I did. The model of the Hydra does generate questions, some of which I address in the book, others left yet to be explored.

Please note that this book is intended for the general reader, not an academic audience. That said, I am a sociologist and used my sociological training to make sense of the many injustices I see. This book represents one person 's journey trying to understand the world and as such is full of conjecture and sometimes overreaching generalizations. So be it. I believe readers can get from this book a sense of how an idea progresses, deepens, and matures over time. Since 2019 when I first conceived of the Hydra model I have listened to the many challenging comments and questions from my students and colleagues. Make no mistake, this book is a collaborative effort that depended upon countless interactions with hundreds of students, colleagues, and humanitarians. That said, I take full responsibility for all the assertions you'll read below, and I will have an open mind regarding your feedback and comment. Creating a more just world for all is an ongoing struggle. As they say in the Zapatista communities in Chiapas, México 'la lucha sigue', the struggle continues.

This book was supposed to be done many months ago, but as I begin to teach a small class of Rohingya and Bangladeshi learners online I realized that I had so much to learn from them about power, privilege, ascribed statuses, and what it means to be in a constant struggle for a more just world. The final chapters of this book were inspired by these learners, and you can see their words and images on nearly every page. It is to these 20 young women and men that I dedicate this book. Each of them displayed amazing resilience, courage, vision, and a profound sense of humanity that I found utterly inspiring and humbling. Most of all I want to acknowledge and thank my Bangladeshi colleague Azizul Hoque who was not only able to translate the Hydra into his own native language of Bangla but into the Rohingya language as well. Thanks go to Jessica Onley and all the staff at Brac University and the Centre for Peace and Justice for bringing me together with Azizul and our learners.

Dedication

It is to the Rohingya and Bangladeshi learners listed below that this book is dedicated.

Mohamad Fahad, Abdullah, Mohammed Nowkhim, Maung Sawyeddollah, Nurul Abser, Mohammad Harun, Mohammed Mirza Nu, Mamed Aray Shad, Shamima, Umme Salma, Md Ahtaram, Ommey Habiba, Omar Khalek, Jannatul Naem, Ma Khin Win, Salah Uddin, Tin Swe, and Ali Jinnah Hussin.

In their honor I will be contributing a major portion of the proceeds from this book to support education efforts in refugee camps.

Confronting Toxic Othering

Table of Contents

Student Foreword
By Sydney Hallisey, Elon '21

As a reader, or especially a student of sociology, you may think you understand privilege. I certainly thought I did as I enrolled in Dr. Arcaro's class. But there's something about a visual, particularly one with metaphorical significance, that has the power to bring a new perspective and a deeper grasp. The Hydra model shows you a form of privilege on each of its heads, depicting each form attached to a body, emphasizing the connections between them and the intersectionality of privilege. The model also shows a living, breathing, growing being, with the ability to remove heads as issues are tackled and for new ones to grow as additional privileging forces are labelled. As our world evolves so does its privileging forces; they are living, breathing, growing, and changing. In all the books I have read and courses I have taken, I have yet to find a better visual representation of privileging forces and intersectionality.

The Hydra model brought a truly new perspective to the way I examine the world. Many of my fellow students shared similar experiences, like Noelle Bates, who said that "viewing privilege through a framework of intersectionality allows for a broader, and thus more comprehensive, understanding of how we benefit from privilege in our daily lives." Caroline Diskin described understanding the Hydra as "one of the first moments of sociological and humanitarian growth that I saw within myself." Another student described how the Hydra helped them finally grasp the concept of intersectionality, and another reflected on the power of the model to open their eyes to their own privilege.

I was introduced to the Hydra model in the spring of 2020. In Dr. Arcaro's *Global Social Problems* course, we were exploring human responses to humanitarian crises all over the world, only to be launched on our own a few weeks into the semester. The COVID-19 pandemic sent us all home and into virtual learning, and we shifted to examining the impact of the pandemic on different areas and groups of people. We learned about humanitarian responses from the aid sector, and the way different communities were tackling these issues with and without international support. As I struggled with my own experiences during our months of quarantine and grappled with loss and change and fear, it was the Hydra that brought me perspective.

I am a white woman from a middle-class family in the United States, enrolled in a private higher education institution. I carry with me the privileges of hetero/cisnormativity, class, ableism, race/ethnicity, and colonialism. Before my experiences in Dr. Arcaro's course, I was certainly aware of my privilege, but the COVID-19 quarantine left me with a great deal of time for reflection. I thought about how difficult this time was for me despite all the privileging forces to which I have access. I considered the conversations we had in class with refugees, activists, and aid workers all over the world, facing a very different side of the pandemic. These lessons, contextualized by the Hydra, grounded and humbled me throughout my COVID-19 experience, changing the way I viewed the crisis and shifting to a more globalized lens.

As we explored the Hydra, we learned about the nuances within the humanitarian aid sector and ethical aid practices that take into consideration the forces of privilege at play. With so many aid workers possessing different privileges than the communities in which they work, it is crucial to recognize those differences and their impact. Seeing the Hydra and its privileges laid out and considering my place in the model, catalyzed the realization of my humanitarian imperative. It doesn't feel right knowing that my privileges give me an edge I didn't earn, and like aid workers contributing ethically to the field, I want to use the tools I have to support others and fight those forces.

Learning about the Hydra model had a huge impact on my life as I developed a deeper understanding of global social problems during the COVID-19 pandemic, and it directly shaped my interests and career path. Dr. Arcaro's lessons inspired me to pursue a career in the human rights field, and I know the visual of the Hydra will always be in the back of my mind, contextualizing each of my cases and interactions. Although you may not find yourself called to the field by the end of this book, there is no doubt in my mind that these concepts will reshape your perspective and will open your eyes to new views. It will help you grasp important concepts, and you will start to notice these forces at play in different areas of your life. That awareness is truly the first step towards attacking and killing the Hydra, and I am glad to have you with us as we fight the body of the beast together.

Introduction

In the summer of 2019, an official from the international humanitarian organization ALNAP contacted me and asked if I would like to be part of a team to give a talk on various privileging forces in the humanitarian sector. The meeting was to be held in Berlin in October 2019, and I put that in my schedule. I had no idea that this would turn out to be a transformative experience for me. Since 2014, I have been blogging about the humanitarian sector and have published two books- *Aid Worker Voices* (2016) and *Dispatches from the Margins of the Humanitarian Sector* (2021). My thoughts on the various privileging forces became a long series of blog posts that you will find collected below.

These chapters are arranged in the order they were originally published allowing the reader to see the evolution of this idea. I owe much to my many students who have provided constant feedback leading me to expand and deepen the concept. An equally important thanks must go to the many humanitarian colleagues I met in Berlin who continue providing support and comment about the idea. Feedback continues, and that is all to say this book is perhaps not yet done, the metaphor certainly not fully explored.

As I write this, the Palestinians in Gaza are being bombed by the Israeli Air Force, and families are being slaughtered mercilessly. A half a world away in Myanmar, democracy demonstrators are being targeted and killed by the government military known as the Tatmadaw. In Northern Ethiopia in the Tigray region, women and girls are being raped, and there are tens of thousands of Internally Displaced People hoping to make it through another day without violence. Though these three events are tragic, countless other humanitarian crises are unfolding in other parts of the world: Syria, Yemen, Central America, and here in the United States.

Many questions come to mind when I reflect on this seemingly endless list of egregious acts of inhumanity. How did humanity arrive at this point in history where systemic violence is so numbingly common? How are humans capable of such inhumane behavior? What are the root causes of these events? How can the tide of history be altered so that these problems can be addressed peacefully with reason and compassion?

This book attempts to offer a conceptual tool -the Hydra metaphor- which can be used to understand the many privileging forces. The Hydra demands that we understand how all the privileging forces have a common body, and that the head of the Hydra interacts with all the others- intersectionality is inferred and stressed when looking at the Hydra.

When I first began to write about the Hydra back in 2019, George Floyd was still alive, and the Black Lives Matter movement was present, but not nearly in the way that it is now in the spring of 2021. I may be overstating things that the world has gotten collectively more 'woke' in the last 18 months, but I would be willing to defend that comment. The power of mass media has grown such that people can communicate around the world and share stories of their struggles. What I describe below is unique only in the metaphor being used, not the basic idea that social injustices have a very long history and are each deeply embedded in all world cultures to one degree or another.

I invite you to read the following chapters with an open mind and a critical eye. The feedback you give will inform future versions of this book.

Chapter 1
The Relevance Question

Blog post originally published October 2019

> *"It seems obvious that relevance should be*
> *a basic test of humanitarian assistance.*
> *If people don't receive what they really*
> *need in a crisis, something is going wrong."*
> —Sophia Swithern, Background Paper for alnap32

Thoughts on Being More 'Relevant' as a
Humanitarian Worker

Being a humanitarian worker often involves navigating between many cultures all while responding to the needs of people experiencing some form of extreme crisis. It is tough work, in part because dealing with 'other' people demands intellectual and emotional effort focused on the critical goal of maintaining relevance. Critical questions related to relevance include:

- Are *my actions* appropriate, ethical, and addressing the real needs of the affected communities?
- How are the *actions of my organization* appropriate, ethical, and addressing heal needs of the affected communities?
- Are the *actions of the humanitarian sector* as a whole appropriate, ethical, and addressing the real needs of the affected communities?

Addressing these questions is not a quick, easy, or a "one and done' process. Mindful reflection on relevance must take into consideration a myriad of factors. Most effectively done, at least some of this reflection should take place in diverse settings where the conversation can include a full range of perspectives, generating new insight on old questions and generating new ones for exploration. One important consideration is how the question of relevance is framed.

Not a Monolith

Before we proceed further, some simple truths: Despite the appearance from 35,000 feet, the humanitarian sector is not a monolithic whole. Humanitarians are not a monolithic whole. Parts of the globe and the peoples who populate them, are not monolithic wholes. Affected communities are demonstratively not monolithic wholes. Donor entities are not a monolithic whole. Nor are any of the above static entities, unchanging and unconnected to the others. The crises that humanitarians respond to are not monolithic, some are 'natural' disasters, others human conflict. Each is very different, and each move along the response, recovery, development continuum at its own pace or not at all.

Hence, though it is obvious to say, none of the above should be treated, either analytically or in practice as if they were static, isolated, or monolithic wholes.

The same can be said of each of us. We are all much more than just our title or the one role we are playing at this moment. We are not static, isolated, or flat, unidimensional beings. By better understanding the complexity in our lives and minds we are better equipped to see complexity in our professional lives as humanitarians. Acting relevant demands nuanced awareness of ourselves and the world in which we live and act.

Must Read for All Humanitarians

In Sophia Swithern's background paper for this year's ALNAP meeting in Berlin entitled "More Relevant? 10 Ways to Approach What People Really Need" she offers deep insights into what she calls the 'relevance question' and provides detailed and insightful analysis on how the question must be framed. Her introduction begins with a clear statement of the problem, and then proceeds to raise some robust observations and questions:

> *It seems obvious that relevance should be a basic test of humanitarian assistance. If people don't receive what they really need in a crisis, something is going wrong. (Page 1)*
>
> *The relevance test raises fundamental questions of knowledge, power and culture. How best to understand*

> *what's most relevant when people's needs are diverse, dynamic, and sometimes at odds with expert views? Who gets the power to decide what's relevant and how? To what extent can humanitarian aid be culturally and contextually relevant, while upholding principles and delivering on time and at scale? Indeed, is it possible for the Western-bred humanitarian system to transcend its origins in order to do so? The relevance test also raises inevitable questions about humanitarian politics, structures, and the resources of the response. Are current systems getting in the way? What kinds of collaboration are possible? And what kind of funding, staffing and expertise would it take to do things better? (Page 4).*

Page seven of her document gives us her working definition for relevance, to wit:

> *... relevance is being in line with the priority needs of affected people.*

Swithern's framing of the question provides tools that we can generate useful, response specific questions and possible solutions. The backbone of her framework of 10 dimensions. She breaks these dimensions down into two categories-understanding and assistance. Each question in turn is refined with a scale depicting the range of possible answers, with one end of the range representing (in most cases) the desired type of answer.

Understanding includes the questions:

How comprehensive is our understanding?

- How inclusive is our understanding?
- How holistic is our understanding?
- How dynamic is our understanding? How polymorphic is our understanding?

Assistance includes these questions:

- How much choice do affected populations have?

- How   tailored is our assistance?
- How co-designed is our assistance with affected people?
- How adaptive is our assistance?
- How complementary is our assistance?

In her concluding remarks, Swithern suggests,

> *If relevance means a close match between response and what people most need, then as we've seen, this forces us to think hard about most aspects of humanitarian action. The relevance test reaches wide and deep.*
>
> *We have seen how relevance and appropriateness are inextricable: The 'what' and the 'how' of humanitarian action are both important if people are to have their needs met – for their tangible priorities such as food, as well as their intangible priorities such as dignity. This takes us beyond simplistic ideas of supply and demand and encourages us to think about humanitarian assistance as much relational as transactional.*
>
> *We have also seen the blurred line between understanding what's relevant and responding to it, that these are iterative rather than discrete processes. And while there is much room for improvement in understanding needs, there is not a simple equation to be drawn between more information 'in' and more relevant response 'out'. This is not only because of limitations in decision-making and prioritization, but also because subjectivity and complexity pose limits to how much we can know and provide what's most relevant.* (Emphasis added)

Perhaps the most important point she makes here is that understanding and responding to questions of relevance is an iterative process. This means that answering the relevance question, done well, means ongoing efforts by those who are in a position to guide a humanitarian response. That raises the very important question of power. Who within the humanitarian ecosystem has the position and privilege to ask these questions about relevance in the appropriate contexts and in a timely fashion? One answer to that question is, well, everyone, including donor entities, humanitarians, and the affected community.

Let us turn now to the questions of position, power, and privilege.

Maximizing Relevance

Below I address a pervasive issue in the humanitarian sector, namely 'othering.' Understanding at a deeper level the process of 'othering' better can make for more relevant actions, at least that is my hope as I invite you to read the remainder of this chapter. By understanding the process of 'othering' relative to all the heads of the Hydra, we can see how privileging forces embed themselves in the norms, policies, and laws that impact individuals and organizations and, seeing interactions based on this lens, make our responses more relevant.

Lessons from the Nataruk Massacre

There is evidence of violence between groups of hunting and gathering bands 10,000 years ago in Kenya that appear to have included:

> 'Extreme blunt-force trauma to crania and cheekbones, broken hands, knees and ribs, arrow lesions to the neck, and stone projectile tips lodged in the skull and thorax of two men.'

Four of them, including a late-term pregnant woman, appear to have had their hands bound.

Ethological evidence indicates that our closest relative, chimpanzees, are quite capable of attacking and killing rivals, providing support for the premise that inter-group enmity is woven into our basic nature. Our tendency to other is evidenced in every corner of the world all through human history.

'Othering' is basic to our species; there has always been an 'us' and 'them'. Perhaps it is best explained as an evolved mechanism functioning to maximize both individual and group fitness, it is an adaptive mechanism. Othering is part of our genetic motherboard.

Othering Explained

Though the exact origin, at least for some, is unclear, many scholars agree one of the earliest uses of the term 'othering' comes from sociologist Edward Said's 1978 classic book *Orientalism*. This term is inclusive of the entire range of marginalizing 'isms' and phobias including (but not limited to) ethnocentrism, racism, fascism, sexism, homophobia, Islamophobia, and so on.

The semantic tool here is that Said has turned a noun into a verb, as in 'to other' someone or some group, to separate them from us.

Perfectly on point, John A. Powell and Stephen Menendian offer a detailed, timely and very informative article entitled "The Problem of Othering: Toward Inclusiveness and Belonging" which begins with this broad, but I think accurate, statement:

> *The problem of the twenty-first century is the problem of 'othering.' In a world beset by seemingly intractable and overwhelming challenges, virtually every global, national, and regional conflict is wrapped within or organized around one or more dimensions of group-based difference. Othering undergirds territorial disputes, sectarian violence, military conflict, the spread of disease, hunger, and food insecurity, and even climate change.*

The quotation below is from an article by S. R. Moosavinia, N. Niazi, and Ahmad Ghaforian comparing *Orientalism* to George Orwell's *Burmese Days* presents the concept and also anticipates some points I'll cover below.

> *Orientalism is closely related to the concept of the Self and the Other because as Said points out in his second definition of Orientalism, it makes a distinction between the Occident, i.e. Self and the Orient, i.e. the Other, since the analysis of the relationship of the 'self' and the 'other' is at the heart of Post-colonialism and many define Post-colonialism in terms of the relationship of the self and the Other. For instance, Boehmer emphasizes that*

'Postcolonial theories swivel the conventional axis of interaction between the colonizer and colonized or the self and the Other'.

As an aside, I recognize the irony that Orwell's *Burmese Days* discusses the origins of one of the most tragic cases of 'othering' burning today in Myanmar and Cox's Bazar. His other notable works *Animal Farm* and *1984* can be seen as a commentary on 'othering', especially so in *Animal Farm* where 'we are all equal, but some are more equal than others.'

Othering 101

In the most basic terms, othering can be explained as follows: If A and B are different, A will posit superiority over B, and if there is an asymmetry of power with A having more, A will impose its will on B.

A can be different from B in many ways, and the most critical variables include various social statuses, most ascribed, i.e., assigned at birth and/or otherwise not chosen. These include (but are not limited to), you guessed it, gender, sexuality, body type, race/ethnicity/tribe, religion, age, social class, ability, and colonial status.

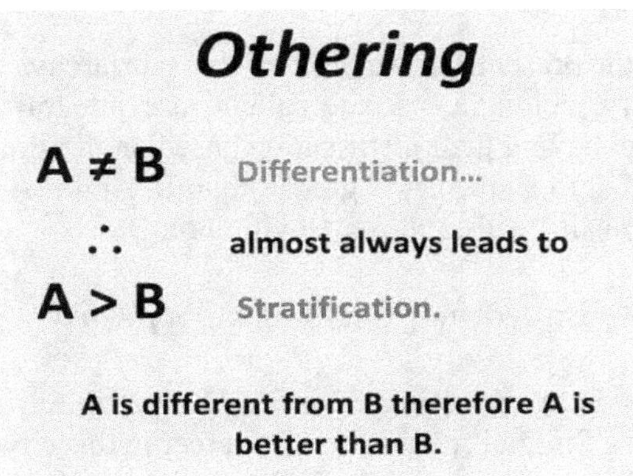

Chart by Tom Arcaro

Key to mention here is that othering can be something done by one person to another person or group *and/or* from one group to another. Indeed, the unit of analysis matters as you get into the weeds describing and understanding othering.

This dynamic, going from "difference/differentiation" to "one is better than the other/stratification" is virtually inevitable when A is more powerful than B. To wit, gender differentiation has, in the vast majority of cultures, always degenerated into gender stratification, oft times toxically so.

Othering is an inclusive, umbrella-like term, and all forms of marginalization are merely variations on this process. When there is a power imbalance the object of othering ('B') tends to be dehumanized, counter-anthropomorphized, having its basic human qualities stripped, and seen as 'less then.'

The 'othering' marginalization process impacts all aspects of the culture such that this dehumanization becomes normalized, baked into every aspect of the culture. When some forms of othering are institutionalized and even celebrated, this can lead to an acceptance of othering in other realms. I am thinking here of the 'national' or 'team' pride that is celebrated at the Olympics internationally and here in the US where, in my case, it is OK to talk trash about Michigan football if you are an Ohio State fan like myself. Indeed, ethnic ('othering') jokes seem to be universal across cultures, and as Gershon Legman points out in his book *No Laughing Matter*. "Under the mask of humor our society allows infinite aggressions, by everyone and against everyone."

Fast forward to the present and we observe that patriarchy, classism/racism, heteronormativity, colonialism/ paternalism, are integral features of our global culture, all having their justification based on the simple thought that if A does not equal to B, then A is greater than B. And if A is stronger than B it can -and typically will- impose its will upon B.

Baked In = Sociological *a prioris*

On a sociological note, that #alnap32 is taking place in Berlin is significant. Sociologist Georg Simmel spent his entire career in this city, and among his major concepts is the idea of sociological *a prioris*. Kant's assumption was that human minds are not born fully unformed or *tabula rasa* but rather come frontloaded with certain built-in *a priori* structures that determine, for example, our concepts of space and time. For his part, Kant has been affirmed and his basic ideas extended by research into evolutionary psychology (as an example the cultural universal of craving sweet, salty and/or fatty foods).

Simmel endorses but also extends Kant by arguing that we live in a social world created by our ancestors, both ancient and even more recent. We live in a world of reified and ossified social structures which we internalize through the process of socialization; they become part of the way we understand, experience and, hence, act in the world. Othering in its many forms is part of the world in which we live and act. Sexism, racism, heteronormativity, just to name a few, have been literally baked into our social and cultural worlds. In some cases, recognizing the more firmly entrenched othering structures demands a fundamental rethinking of our world, and hence our self. Confronting othering means finding ways to de-ossify existing mental and social structures. No small task, that.

Why Othering Persists: The Better and Not So Better Angels of Our Nature

While humans can imagine and even wax poetic about perfect justice, we often act otherwise. Though few would openly disagree, when offered the observation that "we are all God's children", their actions speak otherwise. In US culture we see this clearly within the evangelical movement which openly supports acts and policies that can be seen as racist. In Myanmar, those who talk of following in the path of the Buddha end up perpetuating genocide. How does this duplicity happen?

> May we compete with one another,
> To speak for Thy Creation with more justice—
> Coöperating in this competition
> Until our naming
> Gives voice correctly,
> And how things are,
> And how we say things are
> Are one.

Kenneth Burke's 1939 poem, "Dialecticians Prayer"
Diagram by Tom Arcaro

In sociology we talk about 'ideal culture' and 'real culture.' Ideal culture reflects the better angels of our nature. It is seen in our formal documents and more progressive laws. In the US, the Constitution and Bill of Rights are such documents. Internationally, the Universal Declaration of Human Rights represents such lofty ideals.

The rhetoric of our ideal culture statements is driven, stated in psychological terms, by our superego, our conscience. These are the internalized and culturally accepted values that our religions, teachers, parents, and coaches have imparted on us and represent the positive and cohesive bonds that help maintain (relative) social order.

By contrast, our behavior, that is 'real culture', is driven by a more buried, primal part of our brain and is guided by fear, mistrust and selfish motivations, the 'motherboard' mentioned above. Herein lies the core source of othering.

When Martin Luther King, Jr. tells us in his "We Shall Overcome" speech

> *"We shall overcome because the arc of the moral universe is long, but it bends toward justice."*

… he is saying that our institutions are collectively and slowly getting more progressive and that sometime in the future, we will have a more just world. His assumption that the better angels of our nature-our ability to produce 'ideal culture' laws and structures- will eventually prevail, may be too optimistic. As we watch a world increasingly fueled by toxic nationalism and even outright fascism, the real culture of our othering tendencies seems to be winning this moral tug of war. Calling on Kenneth Burke's poem "Dialectician's Prayer", we must be sober to the fact that that's how things are, and how we say things are, are not one.

Twitter Post: Used with permission from the author Dara Passano.

A Note on 'Brown on Brown' Othering

Though any rank ordering of the most toxic manifestations of othering would be difficult to defend, racism is certainly near the top of any list. Examples of racism-manifesting itself in many ways up to and including genocide-are depressingly easy to find as one scans the globe now and back through history. Many of these examples include inter-tribal (and even intra-tribal) conflicts and evidence of a tribe or group enslaving another. Racism can and has included white on white, white on people of color (POC) and POC on POC. The paradox-and the reality-is that a group can be at the same time the perpetrator of and the object of racism.

Taken up an analytical notch, one person or group being 'othered' and marginalized because of one ascribed status (for example race/ethnicity) does not preclude that same person or group marginalizing and othering based on another ascribed status (for example, sexual expression). And that gets used to the topic of the antidote to othering. In the current vernacular, the term being used is 'woke.'

What does it mean for a humanitarian worker to be 'woke'? Huge -and loaded- question, that.

Status, Privilege and Being 'Woke'

From a humanitarian worker perspective, one very important factor determining comfort in the workplace is how accepted one feels concerning their various social statuses. There are many statuses, both ascribed and achieved (and some a hybrid) that, depending upon the social context, emerge as 'master statuses' which can significantly color how one is viewed, responded to and ultimately either accepted or marginalized both socially and professionally. Among these statuses are gender, age, race/ethnicity, sexual orientation, religion, level of education and outstanding physical attributes. Adding to the complexity is the fact of intersectionality, the complex and inherent interconnection of power and marginalization that impacts everyone either directly or indirectly.

Most of us as activists and humanitarians train ourselves to see beyond the surface (to become 'woke'), but the reality is that life-long socialization into using specific cultural lenses sometimes can make us unaware of some of the assumptions we are making about 'the other'. Recognizing, owning, and then mindfully checking ones' ethnocentrisms and various privileges is rarely a 'one and done' exercise, but rather a lifetime journey, especially for those-humanitarians, for example-who regularly encounter diversity in its many rich and complicated forms. Those with privilege must constantly be not only willing but ever ready to engage in anti-oppressive practices and encourage the same in all our workmates.

On a reflexive - and sociological - note, I'll add that having certain ascribed statuses can make the journey toward 'wokedome' longer and harder (but all the more necessary!). As a cis, straight, 'too male, too pale, and too stale' person, I embrace and, critically, learn from that journey daily through listening to my students, colleagues, and others who are differently privileged than me.

To be clear, privileges come in many forms, including (but not limited to) race, class, gender, sexuality, age, and nationality, and, yes, being from the 'global North.' Can privileges amplify each other if, as in my case, a person has multiple privileged statuses? Of course.

Kimberlé Crenshaw coined the term 'intersectionality' many years ago to help us understand the complex, cumulative way in which the effects of multiple forms of discrimination (such as racism, sexism, and classism) combine, overlap, or intersect especially in the experiences of marginalized individuals or groups.

Perhaps we need a new word to describe the complex, cumulative way in which the effects of multiple privileges combine, overlap, or intersect and thus amplify the power of these privileges in both individuals and groups. Having this word might help us in our never-ending journey toward personal and organizational relevance.

Circling Back to Relevance: Fighting the Hydra

Two main points to conclude. First, understanding 'othering', as I point out above, is never a case of, 'one and done.' Borrowing from Sophia Swithern, we best think of it as an 'iterative' process. I'll add that it is a process that needs to be done mindfully, systematically, and with a constant awareness of the hurdles that lie along the pathways of implementation. Closing the gap between the 'is' and the 'ought' takes constant work.

Concept by Tom Arcaro. Artwork by Ahmed al Fadaam.

Understanding othering (and acting in response to that understanding) is one dimension of being 'woke'. Though the term 'woke' typically applies to an individual, all avatars of the humanitarian ecosystem - individuals at all levels, organizations (including ALNAP), and donor entities of various stripes) can also become more self-aware, more 'woke.' Those in positions of power must have the desire to become constantly more self-aware of their othering and to hone their ability to facilitate this journey among those with which they work. To repeat, this is an interactive process.

Secondly, in her background paper, Sophia Swithern offers many on point questions which demand that the reader understand more clearly power, privilege, and perspective, to look at the humanitarian sector with eyes wide open, looking for and recognizing 'baked in' personal, organizational, and sector-wide structures that marginalize those in the affected community (and perhaps each other). Her lessons shine light on the path forward and highlight the need to see more clearly the impacts of patriarchy, racism, colonialism, classism, paternalism, and hetero/ cisnormativity.

The more that individual humanitarians, humanitarian organizations and donor entities understand the process of othering and how to confront its manifestations, the more relevant their actions will be. Swithern urges us to understand what the affected community really needs. I'll suggest that what people need is to be free from marginalization, from being othered.

A Hydra, the many-headed serpent in Greek mythology, is a good analogy here for 'othering'. This dragon-like beast is immortal - when one of its heads is cut off two more grow in its place. So it is with othering, an ever-present demon that humans must fight that has many toxic manifestations. As humanitarians, this epic battle must be fought first in the service of relevance, of "… in line with the priority needs of affected people." Finally, perhaps we should keep in mind that though fighting these demons individually is a natural impulse, perhaps the body should be attacked most vigorously.

Postscript: Implementation

Not long ago I had the chance to talk with Linda Polman, author of one of the more scathing books about the humanitarian sector, *Crisis Caravan*. We talked about relevance and how the sector could improve. She said,

> *Everybody inside the aid industry knows what should be done. Everybody knows how it could be better. But to implement all those recommendations, that's the problem. To think of how it should be better, how it can be better, is not the difficult part, it's the implementation part.*

True words, those. *Talking* about change ('making our response more relevant') is the easy part. The next step, going from discussion to writing or rewriting policy, procedures or protocol is much more difficult. But words on documents only become action when implementation happens. The fact that the humanitarian sector is an open and highly complex system made up of thousands of bureaucratic entities, each with their ossified structures, makes unilateral implementation a difficult and perhaps Sisyphean task. Coordination among and between all entities within the sector must continue and even intensify; we must all get on (and stay on) the same iterative 'woke bus'.

And that's why meetings like ALNAP are critically important, helping to facilitate and further inter and intra-sector forward progress on critical topics such as relevance. May we all be up to the task, whatever our parts may be.

Confronting Toxic Othering

Chapter 2
ALNAP Comments, Berlin 2019

Blog post originally posted on January 11, 2020

ALNAP Comments, Berlin 2019

Reflections on What It Means
to Be a Humanitarian

Below are the comments I made as part of the 'Jigsaw' session at the October 2019 ALNAP Conference in Berlin. These comments are an alternate version of "The Relevance Question" blog post (https://blogs.elon.edu/aidworkervoices/?p=1500). I made about the conference theme of 'Relevance.'

Berlin. Photo by Tom Arcaro.

After I gave these comments, conference participants were separated into five large groups and each was charged with discussing questions related to one of the five privileging forces, later to report out to the larger group. Here are the questions for each group:

- **Patriarchy** – How do we see patriarchy manifesting in the 10 dimensions of a relevant response?
- **Race and privilege** – Which core beliefs currently present in the humanitarian sector should we question and why?

- **Colonialism and paternalism** – What would it mean in practice to remove paternalism and colonialism from humanitarianism?
- **Heteronormativity and cisgender-normativity** – What would it mean in practice to make humanitarian response more inclusive of people of diverse genders and sexualities?
- **Classism/ class privilege** –How might our class privilege and identity impact the relevance of humanitarian action we have witnessed or been part of?

Jigsaw Exercise Arcaro Comments

Tom Arcaro with ALNAP sign at Conference in Berlin.
Photograph taken by ALNAP Participant.

I'll assume all in this room have wrestled with their definition of the humanitarian imperative. In so doing, you have also talked with the ghosts of Henri Dunant and Florence Nightingale in attempting to clarify basic humanitarian principles, namely humanity, impartiality, neutrality, and independence. Recently, some have suggested that these four principles need a 21stcentury update, and perhaps a special focus on relevance is in order as we imagine these updates. In any case, all humanitarian principles, old or new, begin with the assumption that all human lives have equal worth. Given that premise, our challenge is to discuss the relevance of humanitarian aid, that is, how well our practices honor human needs in times of crisis.

Our question today is, "How can we better understand power and privilege so that we can maximize the relevance of our actions as humanitarians?" The first part of the question, "How can we better understand power and privilege?" has been discussed in depth by anthropologists, sociologists, and political scientists since the beginning of those disciplines nearly 150 years ago, and these questions are critically relevant as we examine how the humanitarian sector has evolved and is now functioning. To be clear, all humanitarians enjoy some level of power and privilege, and by better understanding both our personal privileges and those of our organizations we can better move toward the optimization of our actions.

Numerous privileging forces exist in various ways around the world including within the humanitarian sector. Some of the more deeply rooted are patriarchy, race and privilege, colonialism and paternalism, Heteronormativity and cisgender-normativity, and classism and class privilege. By understanding both the history and the current manifestation of these privileging forces – and by considering that there may be other privileging forces that need to be described- we will be better equipped to address critical relevance questions.

A Hydra, the many-headed serpent in Greek mythology, is a good analogy here for 'privileging forces'. According to mythology, this dragon-like beast is immortal, and when one of its heads is cut off, two more grow in its place. So it is with privileging forces, an ever-present demon humanitarians must fight that has many toxic manifestations. As humanitarians, this epic battle must be fought first in the service of relevance, that is, (to quote from Sophia Swithern's ALNAP background paper), "... in line with the priority needs of affected people." Finally, perhaps we should keep in mind that though fighting these demons individually is a natural impulse, perhaps the body of the Hydra should be attacked most vigorously. I am confident you will find the facilitators of the breakout sessions you are soon to attend are mindful that these privileging forces are all interconnected and even at times create a toxic synergy.

By exploring questions about each entrenched privileging force we can move closer to addressing the issue of relevance.

Hydra: Othering,
Concept by Tom Arcaro, Artwork Ahmad Al Fadaam

The Hydra is ancient; most of these privileging forces are as old as humankind. By exploring questions about each entrenched privileging force, we can move closer to addressing the issue of relevance. There are many important questions to be asked, but here are some examples

Patriarchy: How are the needs of women being met by predominantly male decision makers?

Race and privilege: How can 'white' humanitarians understand the needs of POC or the nuances of ethnic differences?

Colonialism/paternalism: How can donor entities primarily from the Global North respond to the real needs of those in the majority world?

Heteronormativity/cisgender-normativity: In a world dominated by heteronormativity how are the needs of people with diverse sexual orientation, gender identity, gender expression and sex characteristics being addressed?

Classism/class privilege: Given at times extreme social class disparities between humanitarians and the affected community, how are decisions and actions made less relevant by class bias?

Unless you are an LGBTQI+ woman of color from a poor background someplace in the majority world (Global South), at least one of these privileging forces applies to you. My guess is that more than one applies to most. In my case, all of these apply to me as a hetero white male from the US. Because they will hit close to home, the questions that will be raised today about power and privilege will be uncomfortable to discuss. From this discomfort, we hope that honest insights will be shared and that we can proceed forward armed with ideas that reshape our awareness of privileging forces thus making our humanitarian actions ever more relevant. I invite you to listen, learn, share, and challenge yourself and those in your session in the spirit of openness and a common search for growth.

The Outcomes

When the ALNAP participants reassembled after their group discussions, they were asked to address these additional questions:

1. Which privileging force seems the most difficult to confront and why?
2. What one question should participants ask themselves as they continue with the rest of this meeting?
3. Based on discussions from this exercise, what is one step that you as individuals and/or your organization could take right now to make humanitarian response more relevant for affected people?

ALNAP Conference in Berlin, January 2020.
Photo by Tom Arcaro.

Our discussions were lively, and one theme kept re-emerging, namely the need to not just hear but to listen to the voices from the majority world. One of the most powerful of these voices was that of Arbie Baguios, who describes himself as a 'Decolonial Systems-Thinker'. His presentation at

ALNAP focused around four pieces of advice for those in the donor world, namely:

- Fund courageously.
- Trust generously.
- Measure differently.
- Be a bridge, not an expert.

Our work is ongoing and challenging, constantly demanding fresh perspectives and wise voices.

An Updated Definition

I wrote this for "Understanding the Global Experience: Becoming a Responsible World Citizen," 10 years ago:

> *Global citizens understand at a fundamental level that all humans are born with basic rights, share one planet and thus one fate and, further, embrace an ideology of human growth and potential based upon the assumption that all global citizens should work toward creating a global social structure wherein all humans are not only allowed to reach their full potentials intellectual, physical, and spiritual- but are actively encouraged to do so. But, that this fulfilment of human potential is done in such a way as to honor the fact that humans are only one species among many, and that we must live in sustainable harmony with all life forms on the planet. Further, global citizens understand that just as they have certain rights as global citizens, this role entails an array of important responsibilities.*

Based on my experience at the ALNAP conference and my long-term research into the humanitarian sector, I offer this aspirational definition of a humanitarian.

> *Humanitarians understand at a fundamental level that all humans are born with basic rights, share one planet and thus one fate. Those working in the humanitarian ecosystem embrace an ideology of human growth and potential based upon the assumption that humanitarians should work*

toward facilitating social structures wherein every human is not only allowed to reach their full potentials – intellectual, physical and spiritual- but are actively encouraged to do so in ways that place the highest priority on maintaining and enhancing the dignity of each individual, always aware of the complex array of privileging forces in which they and the members of the communities with which they work are enmeshed. Humanitarians keep in mind that this fulfillment of human potential must be done in such a way as to honor the fact that humans are only one species among many, and that we must live in sustainable harmony with all life forms on the planet.

Confronting Toxic Othering

Chapter 3
Privileging Forces

Blog post originally posted on October 23, 2019

> *"...humanitarian action is a top-down, externally driven, and relatively rigid process that allows little space for local participation beyond formalistic consultation. Much of what happens escapes local scrutiny and control. The system is viewed as inflexible, arrogant, and culturally insensitive. This is sometimes exacerbated by inappropriate personal behavior, conspicuous consumption, and other manifestations of the 'white car syndrome.' Never far from the surface are the perceptions that the aid system does not deliver on expectations and is 'corrupted' by the long chain of intermediaries between distant capitals and would-be beneficiaries." (p. 187)*

> *"Humanitarianism started off as a powerful discourse. Now it is a discourse of power, both at the international and at the community level." (p. 190)*
> —Antonio Donini "Humanitarianism, Perceptions, and Power"
> *In the Eyes of Others* (Abu Sada, editor; 2012)

Background

Earlier this month (October 2019) I was honored to be among the 200 plus people gathered in Berlin for the 32nd annual meeting of the Active Learning Network for Accountability and Performance (ALNAP). Established in 1997, ALNAP is an international sector-wide humanitarian network made up of representatives from various related humanitarian organizations and experts who do research in this area.

I served as one of the facilitators in a 'jigsaw" exercise organized to help the participants link the conference theme of 'relevance' to the enduring historical patterns and norms related to patriarchy, race and privilege, classism/class, colonialism and paternalism, heteronormativity and cisgender-normativity privilege.

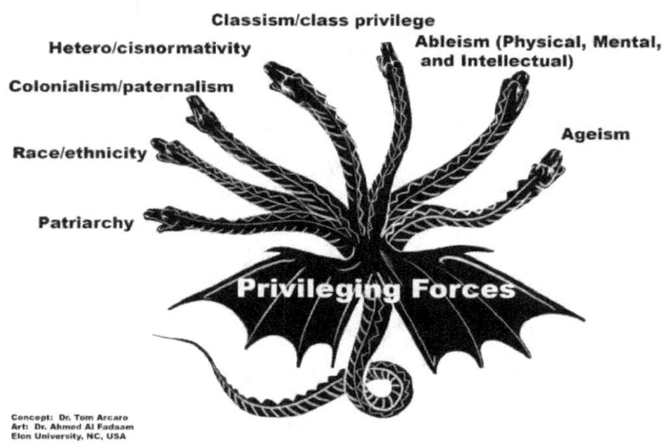

Privileging Forces

My part was to briefly introduce and frame the topics for the breakout sessions related to these five 'privileging forces'. In the days before the conference, I posted the blog "The Relevance Question" where I relevance and observe that each of these five 'privileging forces' have the same origin, namely the universal phenomena of 'othering'. In short, whenever A is different from B and an asymmetry of power exists, there is a tendency for A to assert dominance over B. Stated alternately, social differentiation tends to degrade into social stratification.

In preparation for the conference, I worked with a close friend and colleague (artist and journalist Dr. Ahmed Al Fadaam) to create an illustration that would add depth to my spoken words. As I noted in Berlin,

> *A Hydra, the many-headed serpent in Greek mythology, is*
> *a good analogy here for 'privileging forces'. According to*

mythology, this dragon-like beast is immortal, and when one of its heads is cut off two more grow in its place. So it is with privileging forces, an ever-present demon that humanitarians must fight that has many toxic manifestations. As humanitarians, this epic battle must be fought first in the service of relevance, that is, (to quote from Sophia Swithern's ALNAP background paper), '... in line with the priority needs of affected people.'

Finally, perhaps we should keep in mind that though fighting these demons individually is a natural impulse, perhaps the body of the Hydra should be attacked most vigorously. I am confident you will find the facilitators of the breakout sessions you are soon to attend are mindful that these privileging forces are all interconnected and even at times create a toxic synergy.

Common Process

The idea of a common process underlying these forces comes from an exercise I have done for many years in my classroom when discussing the phenomena of racism. I give this definition:

Racism is an ideology of domination and subordination based on the assumption of biological and/or cultural differences between groups and the use of this assumption to legitimize and/or rationalize the inferior or unequal treatment of one group by another.

I then ask for a definition of sexism, and more astute students will catch on, saying that "Sexism is an ideology of domination and subordination based on the assumption of biological and/or cultural differences between males and females and the use of this assumption to legitimize and/or rationalize the inferior or unequal treatment of females by males." Next, I'll ask for a definition of ageism, or classism, and get similar answers (e.g., "Classism is an ideology of domination and subordination based on the assumption of biological and/or cultural differences of the poor and the use of this assumption to legitimize and/or rationalize the inferior or unequal treatment of the poor by the rich."). The point is clear; all these 'isms' are based on the inexorable process of othering.

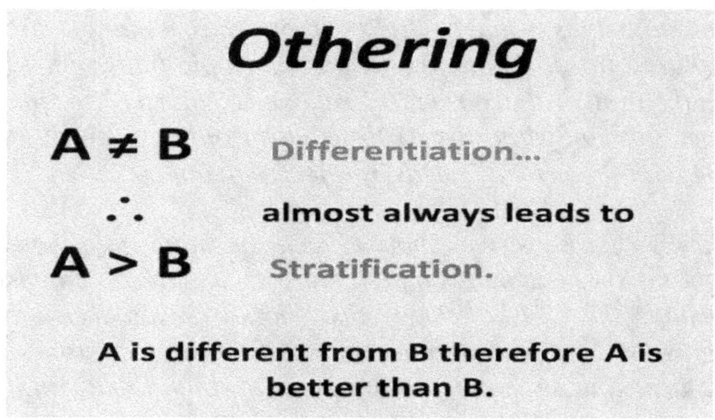

Illustration created by Tom Arcaro

Theory Wonk Observation

In the Wikipedia piece, "Civilization and Its Discontents," Freud asserts *Homo homini lupus* -man is wolf to man- and goes on to say that:

> *The advantage which a comparatively small cultural group offers of allowing this instinct an outlet in the form of hostility against intruders is not to be despised. It is always possible to bind together a considerable number of people in love, so long as there are other people left over to receive the manifestations of their aggressiveness. ... I gave this phenomenon the name of "the narcissism of minor differences."*
> (Source: Sigmund Freud, Civilization and its Discontents, trans. and ed., James Strachey (New York: W. W. Norton, 1961), pp. 58-63.)

Decades later, social critic Erich Fromm extends Freud's work in his book, *The Sane Society*, making use of the phrase 'the lie of civilization', arguing that,

> *Spinoza formulated the problem of the socially patterned defect very clearly. He says: 'Many people are seized by the*

same effect with great consistency. All his senses are so affected by one object that he believes this object to be present even when it is not. If this happens while the person is awake, the person is believed to be insane. ... but if the greedy person thinks only of money and possessions, the ambitious one only of fame, one does not think of them as being insane, but only as annoying; generally, one has contempt for them. But factually greediness, ambition and so forth are forms of insanity, although usually one does not think of them as 'illness.' These words were written a few hundred years ago; they still hold, although the defects have been culturally patterned to such an extent now that they are not even generally thought any more to be annoying or contemptible. (The Sane Society, p.16).

Not Equal

The manifestations of 'othering' which historically (and currently) underlie all the 'privileging forces' mentioned above can be seen as 'socially patterned defects' and are the same as the sociological a priori idea from Georg Simmel (discussed in my post, "The Relevance Question"). I describe these defects as being 'baked in' to the social fabric of nations and cultures all over the world, with the humanitarian sector being no exception. The task before us is to reject the rhetoric made famous by the American 'founding father' Thomas Jefferson, namely that "all men are created equal." Humans are diverse in many ways, some of these differences are rooted in our genes and others in socially constructed realities (many seated in and exasperated by the institution of religion) which have created differences and provided ample opportunities for toxic 'othering.' The quest for a world marked by more justice must aggressively confront the process of othering; doing otherwise will only serve as a frustrating exercise on cutting off one head with two more taking its place.

Counting Heads

The original Hydra image we created had five heads, but we soon realized that more were needed, with the current draft having seven heads which includes the addition of ableism and ageism.

As the jigsaw exercises were processed at the ALNAP gathering, a common refrain was that each privileged force was (1) entrenched in not just global cultures but as well within the humanitarian ecosystem, and (2) though each has its manifestation, these forces all impact each other and hence make, (3) dealing with each separately the wrong approach. All must be addressed holistically and at their root. I'll repeat, othering must be confronted. To extend the discussion, one can see the heads of the hydra -patriarchy, classism, racism, colonialism/paternalism, hetero/cisnormativity, ableism, and ageism - as each themselves a hydra. Each has numerous manifestations in different parts of the world. For example, the many faces of patriarchy present themselves in all manner of guises.

Our task in recognizing and then fighting all these hydras is, perhaps, never ending. But as humanitarians what could be more relevant than fighting for all humanity?

Chapter 4
Humanitarian Principles and Intersectionality

Blog post originally posted on November 2019,
updated January 2020

All Human Lives Have Equal Worth

Humanitarian principles, however, broadly defined, begin with the assertion that all human lives have equal worth. Given that premise, our challenge is to understand the social forces that are a threat to that assumption and frequently lead to humanitarian crises.

In the previous chapters "The Relevance Question" and "Privileging Forces" I discuss how the process of 'othering' is universal, and throughout history has inexorably led to the entrenchment and ossification of many 'privileging forces' that continue to have a massive impact on all global cultures and, necessarily, impact the functioning of the humanitarian ecosystem. I argue that fighting each of these privileging forces individually may seem both necessary and logical, but that to be most effective we must, metaphorically, fight the body of the Hydra, i.e., the process of othering itself. Othering fuels the Hydra's body and thus all its heads.

A more just world will be achieved when we acknowledge and honor our differences and simultaneously counter all arguments (and 'baked in' social, political, and cultural institutions, norms, policies, and laws) that allow social status differentiation to degenerate into stratification, that is, which justify one status being privileged above another. On a conceptual level, I argue this struggle cannot be unidimensional and/or only focus on one location, situation, or issue, but rather needs to employ the concept of intersectionality. That said, it must be granted that on a practical level for any individual at any one point in time, the fight for justice may be specific to one head of their Hydra and that the implementation of any changes must be incremental, specific, and local. Addressing privileging forces is neither fast nor easy. But fundamental social change never is.

Intersectionality

I take as my inspiration for this discussion, the canonical 1989 article "Demarginalizing the Intersection of Race and Sex: A Black Feminist Critique of Antidiscrimination Doctrine, Feminist Theory and Antiracist Politics" by Kimberlé Williams Crenshaw. In this essay, she coined the term 'intersectionality' which has now taken its place among the core concepts in most discussions concerning social justice. She states:

> *This focus on the most privileged group members marginalizes those who are multiple-burdened, and obscures claims that cannot be understood as resulting from discrete sources of discrimination. I suggest further that this focus on otherwise-privileged group members creates a distorted analysis of racism and sexism because the operative conceptions of race and sex become grounded in experiences that represent only a subset of a much more complex phenomenon.*

Photo by Mohamed Bardano, Mohamed Badarne.

Her phrase 'multiply burdened' is apt, and a bit later in the article she explains:

> *Because the intersectional experience is greater than the sum of racism and sexism, any analysis that does not take intersectionality into account cannot sufficiently address the particular way black women are subordinated.*

Our challenge is to take her phrase " … the intersectional experience is greater than the sum of racism and sexism" and add in all of the other 'isms' that make up the heads of the Hydra seen in this illustration.

I must add that most of what I discuss in this, and my two previous posts was addressed in rich detail by sociologist Patricia Hill Collins in her 1990 book, *Black Feminist Thought: Knowledge, Consciousness and the Politics of Empowerment*. The reader is encouraged to read both Crenshaw and Hill's works for a better understanding of intersectionality.

Multiply Privileged

In this chapter, I offer a flipped view of Crenshaw's discussion and explore the many complexities related to the idea of 'multiple privileges.' At least one or more of these privileges are possessed by all humanitarians.

One exercise we can do is list our privileges. Using myself as an example, (moving from left to right on the Hydra) I am male, white, from the 'Global North', straight, living in the upper-middle class, mentally stable and physically able and old, but not quite elderly. I am 'status positive' all the way around. Keeping this all very binary and allowing either a zero or one on each of the seven heads, my score would be a 6.5 out of seven (I am starting to feel the subtle signs of marginalization as I near retirement). What is your total privilege?

Note: Two points. First, each of the seven privileges represented are not binary, and a more thorough discussion would list each, expanding on the shades of privilege possible. Secondly, I am aware that there are other privileging forces, some general and others more culturally or situationally specific. Please bear with me as I proceed with this narrower view.

Privilege comes from perceived social status. Considering our Hydra and the seven privileging forces illustrated (patriarchy, race/ethnicity, colonialism/ paternalism, ableism, heterosexual/ cisnormativity, aaclassism/class privilege, and ageism), we can view individuals as having an array of social statuses. Most social statuses are ascribed, i.e., granted at birth. Some statuses are achieved and can be earned (e.g., training or educational degrees or getting hired for a job). For all of us, both kinds of statuses, ascribed and achieved, impact directly how the privileging forces act upon us during our lives.

In the Eye of the Beholder

Here we must include the concepts 'master status' and 'identity management.' All individuals possess an array of statuses, but in any specific social setting one status may become more important than the others, i.e., their situational 'master status.' Restated, one's master status is fluid, and is relative to the specific social setting; it is what the others in the context view as your most salient feature.

For example, if you are white female in a room full of POC females, your gender may be less relevant than your race; your race is your master status in this context. Identity management is critical when examining those statuses which can be hidden or are otherwise not visually apparent. A case in point is that in many circumstances, one's sexuality can be disclosed or not disclosed as a matter of choice by the individual, that is, in some cases, we can manage our identity with regards to those statuses which are not readily apparent. Other examples are one's religion (or lack thereof), national origin, social class, mental illnesses, etc.

Using the equation below, it is possible to give yourself a privilege score, overall and in a typical work context, based on your various statuses.

An individual's total privileging forces are a function of the intersection between one's position vis-a-vis the various privileging forces of patriarchy, privilege, ableism, race/ethnicity, classism/class, ageism, colonialism/paternalism, and heterosexual/cisnormativity. In short form, TP = f(P*R*C*H*Cl*Ab*A), where TP = total privilege, and the remaining letters in the formula represent the various heads of the Hydra. Anyone's TP will vary dramatically over time with the weight given to each variable depends upon the sociocultural context.

Consider how your score changes depending upon the interactional context, even as you move from one part of your day to the next. The best we can do in any one moment is to (1) be aware of our privilege score overall, (2) understand both the immediate and longer-term social contexts in which we function, (3) understand how our privileges are perceived by those with which we are interacting, (4) and work to acknowledge relative privileges and how these may impact the interactions. We must constantly 'take the role of the other' and imagine what they see when they see us, and most importantly, what they perceive as our master status.

Checking Your Privileges

Most are familiar with the concept of white privilege, and, if they present as 'white', know to be mindful of the privilege that comes from this status. To an equal extent, I'll presume, most are aware of male privilege and the need to check the same. As we go through the heads of the Hydra, each comes with a corresponding 'privilege'. Hetero privilege, class privilege, able privilege, age privilege, and so on. All of these must be in the vocabulary of those wishing to be sensitive to the various privileging forces.

Perhaps the most relevant for many humanitarians is the 'Global North' privilege. Though most humanitarians globally are from the majority world (also referred to as the 'Global South'), many work for INGOs that are (still) headquartered in the Global North, though this may be changing in part as a reaction to the Grand Bargain agreed to in 2016. Key here is understanding the importance of unit of analysis, i.e., whether one is considering the individual or the organization in which the person works.

All humanitarians need to ask themselves questions about status and privilege, but it is also important to think in terms of one's organization. The reflexive question, 'am I being paternalistic (racist, homophobic, etc.)?' must be asked. But equally important, and in terms of sector-wide change, critical, is the question, 'is my organization being paternalistic (etc.)?' In the vernacular of sociology, we must pay attention to both units of analysis.

Putting It All Together

The table below offers a summary. Down the vertical axis are the privileging forces and along the horizontal are several questions that can be asked of each.

Privileging force	Social status correlate; HPS	Can be typically 'managed'?	Life chances (long term) relevance	Situational relevance	Intersectional synergy potential	Future trajectory
Patriarchy	Gender; male	No	Yes	High	High	Slowly getting better (?)
Race/ethnicity	Race; white	No	Yes	High	High	Slowly getting better (?)
Colonialism/paternalism	Location of birth; Global north	Sometimes	Yes	Medium	High	Slowly getting better (?)
Heterosexual/cisnormativity	Sexuality; cis-heterosexual	Yes	Yes	Low (?)	Variable/High	Slowly getting better (?)
Classism/class privilege	Social class; middle to upper class	Yes, mostly	Yes	Medium	Variable/High	Slowly getting better (?)
Ableism	Physical/mental abilities; able and healthy	Varies	Yes	Medium	High	Slowly getting better (?)
Ageism	Age; older	No	N/A	Medium	Variable/High	Slowly getting worse (2)

Note: HPS = historically privileged status

All the cells have been filled in tentatively and with a full realization that changes will be (should be) suggested by colleagues and critics; this table is a starting point for discussion.

From left to right this table breaks down the *Privileging forces*, (1) the social status correlates to this force (and gives the historically privileged status), (2) questions whether the status can be managed, (3) assesses the long term life relevance for the individual, (4) assesses the situational relevance, (5) gauges the 'intersectional synergy potential', and finally (6) makes a projection as to the prospects are for social change to minimize or eliminate each privileging force.

Keeping in mind Crenshaw's point that each force does not simply add on to the others but rather interacts and creates a multiplicative effect, the 'intersectional synergy potential' is the category that cries out for more clarification and explanation, perhaps in another post.

As for the future trajectory, the most desired outcome is that in the future, once we have fully understood and defused the process of othering, all these privileging forces will be neutralized.

All the above are draft ideas, not ready for prime time, just the opposite. I offer these thoughts hoping that others will actively critique the scheme I have proposed. And that is how productive discussions evolve: dialectically and through back-and-forth discussion. A thesis generates antithesis, and the tension created yields a synthesis which itself may generate a new antithesis and subsequent new syntheses. Iterative dialogue is critical, vital, and the only productive pathway forward.

Humanitarian Principles and Intersectionality

Above I have argued an obvious point, namely that humanitarian principles begin with the assumption that all lives have equal value and that the process of othering gives rise to an array of privileging forces that are inherently anti-humanistic/ humanitarian. Most humanitarians are 'multiply privileged' and thus face a challenge regarding how to be proactive in first understanding their statuses and then in addressing this power asymmetry in their actions (1) as individuals, colleague to colleague and (2) when interacting with the beneficiary community. Humanitarians must also be keenly aware of the power differentials between their organization and the organizations with which they work, and that, if working for a Global north based INGO (or other organization, e.g., UN), their master status may be at times that of 'INGO official.'

Mindful progress forward addressing all the heads of the Hydra means *addressing the entire othering process*, not an easy or simple job for those with high overall privilege scores. I suggest we all take lessons from those with lower overall privilege scores, making a special effort to learn from those like Kimberlé Crenshaw hailing from the academic world and, better yet, from those within their organizational ranks.

Chapter 5
The Gaping Hole in the Hydra Model:
Religious Persecution

Blog post originally posted on November 29, 2019
Updated February 1, 2020

> *Religion is arguably one of the most egregious 'othering' forces
> that have ever existed. All through recorded history people have
> been marginalized - and in countless cases murdered - because
> they were of the 'wrong' religion." "The normal and the
> stigmatized are not persons, but perspectives."*
> -Erving Goffman, *Stigma*, 1963

Prologue

As I write this, Myanmar's Daw Aung San Sun Kyi and her team are preparing to respond to The Cour Pénale Internationale (International Criminal Court) formal charges of genocide against the Muslim Rohingya at the International Court of Justice at The Hague. The world will be watching these proceedings, and we as a global community must continue demanding justice be served and the dignity of all humans is defended.

Review and Context

In Chapter 7, "Humanitarian Principles and Intersectionality," I talked about both ascribed and achieved statuses, how these are tied to the process of othering, and the inevitability that this process leads to the rise of various 'privileging forces', namely, patriarchy, privilege, ableism, race/ethnicity, classism/class, colonialism/paternalism, heteronormality/cisnormativity, and ageism. My suggestion was that we should all be aware of the processes underlying the generation and perpetuation of various 'privileging forces' that impact everyone on the planet.

The Hydra image used to illustrate these forces, I argued, was a work in progress. Indeed, one of the most egregious and age-old tools of 'othering' is left out of this image, or at least not amplified properly. That force is religion.

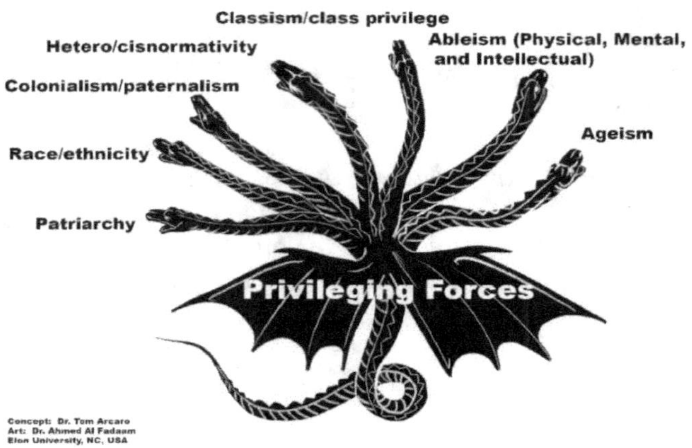

As a sociologist, I know that religion is a cultural universal and that one of the most important elements of many humans' self-identity is their status vis-a-vis some faith tradition. Where does religion fit into this drawing?

There are many religions - Muslim, Zoroastrian, Jew, Catholic, Hindu, Buddhist, Protestant, and the list goes on. Increasingly, to be inclusive we must also include the status 'non-believer.' Everyone has a religious status, that is clear, and that status impacts how the individual feels about themselves, but more importantly, it impacts how the person is seen by others. At times, one's status relative to religion becomes the master status, the one most salient.

Some statuses are obvious, like age and, in many cases, race. These statuses are apparent to everyone as soon as they see your face. Other statuses can be hidden, disclosed at will. One's sexuality, for example, can remain private. The same is true for one's religion, though at times religion is presumed by ethnicity or other factors.

The Gaping Hole in the Hydra Model:
Religion as a Tool of Persecution

Religion is arguably one of the most egregious 'othering' forces that has ever existed. All through recorded history, people have been marginalized- and in countless cases murdered - because they belonged to the 'wrong' religion. The list of examples here is long, bloody, and full of hypocrisy. The crusades. The holocaust. Use of the Christian Bible to justify slavery, racism, homophobia, and misogyny in the US and virtually everywhere else around the globe. Groups who misuse the Koran to perpetuate violence against all 'infidels': ISIS, Boko Haram, Al-Qaeda, Al-Shabaab.

But there can be something as bad as being of the 'wrong' religion, and that is being an atheist. In 2014, the Pew Research Center found that laws restricting apostasy and blasphemy are the most common in the Middle East and North Africa, where 18 of the region's 20 countries (90 percent) criminalize blasphemy and 14 (70 percent) criminalize apostasy. While apostasy laws exist in only two other regions of the world – Asia-Pacific and Sub-Saharan Africa – blasphemy laws can be found in all regions, including Europe (in 16 percent of countries) and the Americas (29 percent).

Looking at history we can see a pattern, namely in any nation or region the religion of those in power is frequently used as a justification for oppression and even genocide against those not of their faith. Here are just a few recent examples:

- Hindus marginalizing Muslims in India.
  https://www.aljazeera.com/news/2019/04/24/in-indias-democracy-muslims-feel-increasingly-marginalised.
- Muslims marginalizing all non-Muslim is in ISIS-controlled areas.
  https://www.theatlantic.com/magazine/archive/2015/03/what-isis-really-wants/384980/.
- Jews marginalizing Muslims in Palestine.
  https://www.aljazeera.com/news/2019/04/24/in-indias-democracy-muslims-feel-increasingly-marginalised/37c3673c1
- Christians marginalizing Muslims in the US.
  https://www.newamerica.org/in-depth/anti-muslim-activity/.
- Muslims marginalizing atheists in Bangladesh.
  https://www.bbc.com/news/blogs-trending-34338691.

- Confucians marginalizing Muslims in China. https://www.cfr.org/backgrounder/chinas-repression-uighurs-xinjiang.
- Buddhists marginalizing Muslims in Myanmar. https://news.un.org/en/story/2018/08/1017802/.https://www.bbc.com/news/blogs-trending-34338691

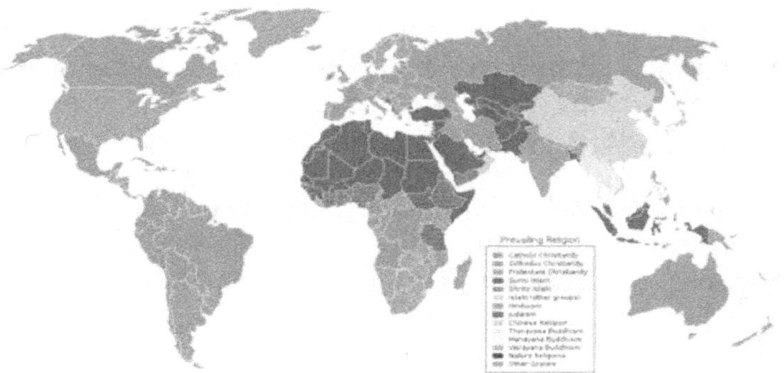

Prevailing World Religions. By LilTeK21 at English Wikipedia.

The US-based Pew Research Center has been tracking restrictions based on religion and had this to say:

> *Over the decade from 2007 to 2017, government restrictions on religion – laws, policies and actions by state officials that restrict religious beliefs and practices – increased markedly around the world. And social hostilities involving religion – including violence and harassment by private individuals, organizations, or groups – also have risen since 2007, the year Pew Research Center began tracking the issue.*

The number of nations with restrictions rose from 40 in 2007 to 52 in 2017. Being in the religious minority, wherever you are in the world, is never easy and can oftentimes be fatal.

In *Fuck Religious Rules and Wars*on YouTube, Rebel Riot addresses religious othering that many, particularly atheists, might agree with. This song/video, by the Burmese punk band Rebel Riot, is a blanket condemnation of all violence based on religious differences.

Religion as a Privileging Force

Referring back to the Hydra, it is easy to see that religion has been used as an amplifying force by many of the heads. It has reinforced sexism and misogyny (patriarchy), been used to justify racism and ethnic hatred, it was used amply and often by colonizing forces to subjugate, control, and mollify. In many cultures, religion has been used to persecute non-heteronormative or cis-normative individuals, it has been used as a tool to placate the poor and have them accept a life of suffering, and more so in earlier historical periods, was used to marginalize the physically or mentally disabled. The outlier head on the Hydra in this respect is ageism, where religion tends to support and honor elders.

All the privileging forces amplify each other in a myriad of ways, but religion seems to be in a class by itself in terms of its toxic potential. Reading and/or watching debates on the question as to whether the net impact of religion is positive or negative is instructive, with those who argue in favor of the 'net negative' impact have much to say about how religion has often been used to justify 'othering' (see chapter on "Privileging Forces" and subsequent marginalization).

A major complicating factor is the fact that religion and ethnicity are often woven together in complex cultural ways. A classic example is those who are ethnically/culturally Jewish but choose not to subscribe to the Jewish religion. Similarly, many are ethnically/culturally Muslim but are otherwise non-religious. This conflation of religion and ethnicity is, indeed, a somewhat universal phenomenon.

Relevant to All Humans and Humanitarians

One basic truism in sociology is that who we are is a function of who is seeing us, i.e., our social context; we are as others perceive us. As Erving Goffman put it in his book *Asylums,*

> *The self in this sense is not a property of the person to whom it is attributed, but dwells rather in the pattern of social control that is exerted. .... This special kind of institutional*

> *arrangement does not so much support the self as constitute it.* (1961: p. 168)

Taking a look at a (non-existent) 'typical humanitarian', she/he moves through an array of social contexts, each a different audience. Just a few of these audiences relevant to the workplace include:

- Superiors (bosses and bosses of bosses).
- Peers (those at the same level).
- Subordinates.
- Members of the affected communities (if relevant).

Though there are important exceptions, as a matter of individual impression management, one's status vis-a-vis religion can be shared or hidden in various social settings. To complicate things even further, presenting oneself as a member of one faith or another (or no faith) is frequently easy to do. As a species, we are quite adept at lying to each other (and even to ourselves) when there is some benefit to be reaped.

Depending on where a humanitarian worker is deployed, their religious status may need to be shared, not shared, or lied about. Imagine a Jewish humanitarian being deployed to the Middle East, an atheist being sent to Bangladesh, or a Sunni Muslim being assigned to work in a Shia controlled area. Humanitarian workers must consider how they will be seen in all contexts and respond accordingly.

Last Thoughts on Religion

Religious status can be rendered minimally important by both individuals and by organizations through actions, policies, and effective impression management. Most major faith based INGO's understand that to be effective, overt displays of their religiosity must remain restricted to high-level insiders and closed settings. World Vision, for example, is a Christian faith-based INGO but has a long history of being a major player in most humanitarian responses around the globe, earning trust even in the Islamic world by effectively presenting themselves and their efforts as religiously neutral, the very opposite of proselytizing.

That said, circumstances can arise, typically in times of conflict or stress, when religious status can define anyone and any organization, making them a target. Perhaps, yes, the Hydra needs to have some representation of the powerful force of religious persecution.

Chapter 6
The Ultimate Goal of the Hydra Is Genocide

Blog post originally posted on December 2019

> *"It is not power that corrupts but fear."*
> −Aung San Suu Kyi, from *Freedom from Fear*.
> Nobel Peace Prize recipient and defender
> of Myanmar's genocidal actions.

This Is an Important Week

This week as I am writing this, there is a Brexit vote in the UK and impeachment hearings against President Trump in the US. These two events are consequential, to be sure, but perhaps no more so than what will be happening in the Netherlands.

Aung San Suu Kyi, State Counsellor of Myanmar.
Photograph by Claudia Truong-Ngoe.

Brought up on charges of committing genocide by The Gambia, Myanmar goes on trial in front of the International Court of Justice. Heavy, somber, and immensely powerful words, those.

In anticipation of the hearing in The Hague, I spent part of this afternoon reading the 46-page document outlining Gambia's case against Myanmar for the genocide against the Rohingya. It begins,

> *In accordance with Articles 36(1) and 40 of the Statute of the Court and Article 38 of the Rules of Court, I have the honour to submit Application instituting proceedings in the name of the Republic of The Gambia ("The Gambia") against the Republic of the Union of Myanmar ("Myanmar"). Pursuant to Article 41 of the Statute, the Application includes a request that the Court indicate provisional measures to protect the rights invoked herein from imminent and irreparable loss.*
>
> *This Application concerns acts adopted, taken, and condoned by the Government of Myanmar against members of the Rohingya group, a distinct ethnic, racial, and religious group that resides primarily in Myanmar's Rakhine State. These acts, which include killing, causing serious bodily and mental harm, inflicting conditions that are calculated to bring about physical destruction, imposing measures to prevent births, and forcible transfers, are* **genocidal in character** *because they are intended to destroy the Rohingya group in whole or in part. They have been perpetrated* **in manifest violation of the 1948 Convention on the Prevention and Punishment of the Crime of Genocide (the "Genocide Convention").** *(Emphasis added)*

The Hydra Wants Blood

There is much to say about the particulars of the Rohingya genocide case, but I want to address a larger issue, the fact that now, in 2019, humanity is still dealing with this grotesque phenomenon. How is it that overt and extreme racism continues to be normalized among our 'civilized' nations? As I search for answers, I am reminded of the words of Erich Fromm who, in his book *The Sane Society*, used the phrase 'the lie of civilization.' His point is simple but clear. Though we are more technologically advanced and are making 'progress' in terms of our control over nature, as a species we are getting less, not more civilized as in being more 'civil' toward each other.

International Court of Justice.
Photo released by the International Court of Justice.
Originally uploaded by Yeu Ninje at en.wikipedia.

The Hydra wants blood and uses fear to induce those in power to orchestrate prolonged, systematic, and brutally effective pogroms, genocides by another name.

Social philosophers throughout history have grappled with the problem of human nature and our species' tendency to fear others. Here now in the 21st century, we are still incapable of controlling this base urge. And so, the Myanmar military, the 'Tatmadaw' went full bore, enthusiastically, about the task of dealing with the 'Bengali' problem. The dehumanization of the Rohingya did not start with the 1982 Burma Citizenship Law, but the embedded privileging forces of race, ethnicity, and religion ultimately fed the Hydra the blood meal it craved. Not unlike Rwanda. Not unlike Cambodia. Not unlike Bosnia. Not unlike 1930/40's Germany.

My point is painfully obvious. The logical extension of unchecked ethnocentrism, racism, and nationalism is genocide. And humanity has yet to figure out how to permanently blunt this deadly process. The Myanmar case before the International Court of Justice is a critical moment in the evolution of our 'civilization.'

For an op-ed on this topic that I co-authored with Zayed Jack, a Rohingya refugee living in Cox's Bazar, read "The Story of Esoup: A Victim of Persecution."

Chapter 7
Yet Another Head on the Hydra?

Blog post originally posted on January 2020

Looks Matter

In the 2016 movie *Whiskey Tango Foxtrot*, Tina Fey plays an embedded journalist in Afghanistan. The phrase '4-10-4' is used by a marine commander as he admonishes the Tina Fey character not to fraternize with his men. The '4-10-4' phrase refers to the old misogynist trope that we rate each other on attractiveness, much more so males rating females rather than the opposite, and that this rating is done on a 1-10 scale, 10 being highly desirable.

The commander's point is obvious, that attractiveness is a matter of context, such that back in New York City, a woman that would be rated a four, in Kabul would be rated much higher, even a ten by the US (and coalition) military personnel.

This is not a new topic among social scientists and other academics. That attractiveness-and particularly female attractiveness-is a factor in social interaction is the subject of Deborah Rhode's 2010 book, *The Beauty Bias: The Injustice of Appearance in Life and Law*, which spawned the term 'lookism'. A new and perhaps useful term.

Lookism refers to differential treatment based on physical appearance. Rhodes argues this is an overlooked form of discrimination in American society, and that it functions in the same manner as other major 'isms' like racism and sexism. My sense at this point is that, yes, based on social science data, looks do matter, of course.

This is most decidedly not just an 'American' thing; lookism is as old as our species in the sense that 'beauty' equates to fitness, and sexual selection as an evolutionary force is quite powerful. To wit: global spending on beauty products is expected to reach USD 863 billion by 2024. By contrast, in 2018 only USD 28.9 billion was spent globally on humanitarian aid, orders of magnitude less than spent on beauty. Let that sink in.

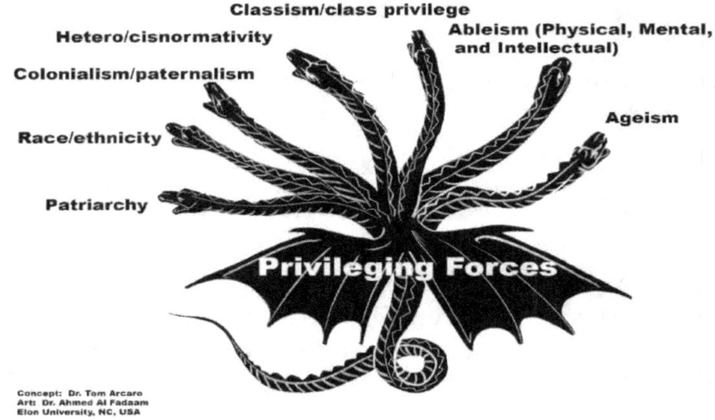

Another Hydra Head?

Have we identified another head on the Hydra? Likely not. As we look at the privileging factors, it seems logical to locate 'lookism' as a subset of ableism. No credible data exists as to what degree 'attractiveness' or looks are a factor in the hiring and/or promoting humanitarian workers, but the number is certainly not zero.

Putting the attractiveness rating aside, let's explore further the general principle that one's status is a matter of context.

Can We Use the 4-10-4 Rating System with Other Statuses?

Allow me to tell on myself with an illustration from my past. In the last 30 years, I have traveled extensively through my university and for research. Early in my career, I traveled to rural India. In the United States, I am very middle-class but in the context of the places I have traveled in rural India I am extraordinarily wealthy.

Just driving into the village, I go from a '6 or 7' to a 10 (or 15)" (*Whiskey Tango Foxtrot*), so to speak. Being seen as extremely wealthy (and by extension) powerful by others, in retrospect, felt good, especially for a person who grew up in abject poverty like me. Could this artificial boost in social status phenomena be a factor in why some from the 'Global North' get into the humanitarian sector?

The takeaway from this post is that mental work done by most humanitarians in a typical day is enormous, and part of that work is necessarily identity management and social-context awareness. Above, I have identified two of the Hydra heads (ableism and class) and argued how these statues are clearly a matter of context. Being aware of one's privileges takes constant work, but this is work that is critical as we deepen our efforts to confront the heads of the Hydra.

Chapter 8
A Code of Ethics for Privileged Anti-Othering Persons: The Humanitarian Imperative and Hydra Revisited

Blog post originally posted on June 29, 2020.
Updated April 30, 2021

Overview

Below I expand on previous posts related to the humanitarian imperative, the privileging forces' Hydra, and the quest for global social justice. Studying and engaging with humanitarians all over the world has provided me with a broad base of insights, and I especially thank those from the majority world (aka Global South) who have so patiently offered me their thoughts, feelings, and opinions.

The recent re-emergence of a surprisingly inclusive movement, #BlackLivesMatter," both here in the US and around the world has many talking frankly about systemic racism and toxic white nationalism, and these conversations have generated action. One perhaps not insignificant example of change is the fact that NASCAR, the auto racing organization that is most popular in the US Southeast has recently banned confederate flags at sanctioned events. These flags have long been a racist symbol and commonly found in abundance at NASCAR races. This change was initiated by one black driver and then embraced by the policy makers in NASCAR. A second and related example is that Mississippi appears to be on the verge of changing its long divisive flag, deleting the confederate flag embedded in the upper corner. [Note: Now has changed.]

Within the humanitarian sector, there are #BlackLivesMatter conversations being held. In the "For More Information" chapter below, you will find the statement by MSF-USA describing racism as a public health crisis. MSF International's position is similar, admitting that the organization had 'failed to tackle institutional racism,' but noting that, "We get a lot of 'all lives matter' reaction from colleagues from different parts of the world. … context is everything."

The deep intersectionality between racism and colonialism embedded within the humanitarian sector needs very close scrutiny and eventually aggressive action at every level, especially within the UN organizations and 'big box' INGO's like World Vision, Oxfam, and others. The seriousness and scale of this self-examination and policy change must be even more progressive and soul-searching that was done in reaction to the Oxfam (and others) #MeToo crisis.

Many are now learning both old and new lessons about how deeply racism is baked into the US (and global) culture, and most are seeking ways to join the movement directly and productively toward true racial justice. JLove Calderon and Tim Wise offer this statement in an article titled, "Code of Ethics for White Anti-Racists."

> *We are persons classified as white in this society. As aspiring anti-racist allies/ collaborators, we seek to work with people of color (and follow their leadership) to create real multiracial democracy. We do not fight racism on behalf of people of color, or as an act of charity. We oppose white supremacy because it is an unjust system, and we believe in the moral obligation to resist injustice.*

This statement, all of it, spoke to me, and I immediately related it to the lessons I have been learning while listening to humanitarians from the majority world. Without using the phrase, they critique the 'white savior complex' and voice support for a humanitarian perspective. Read my blog, "The White Savior Complex" about what some of the respondents said on our survey of humanitarians from the majority world and for further observations about the 'White Savior Complex.'

Over 30 years ago, Kimberlé Crenshaw presented us with the conceptual tool of intersectionality. In the 2017 article, "Kimberlé Crenshaw on Intersectionality, More Than Two Decades Later," she reflects,

> *Intersectionality is a lens through which you can see where power comes and collides, where it interlocks and intersects.*

Humanitarian principles and intersectionality are a critical topic as efforts to make structural, permanent change regarding all privileging forces multiply and mature.

So, with deep gratitude to Calderon and Wise, I offer here a "Code of Ethics for Privileged Anti-Othering Persons," addressing all seven heads of the Hydra.

> *We are persons classified as privileged in our global society. As aspiring anti-patriarchal, anti-racist, anti-ableist, anti-colonial, anti-hetero/cis-normativity, anti-classist, and anti-ageist allies/collaborators, we seek to work with people differently privileged (and to follow their leadership) to create a more just world where all humans have pathways to dignity. We do not fight these privileging forces on behalf of those marginalized, or as an act of charity. We oppose privileging forces because they create unjust systems, and we believe in the moral obligation to resist injustice.*

The fact that these privileging forces are woven deep into the fabric of all modern global cultures and that they 'interlock and intersect' with each other makes confronting them difficult. Like cancer, these privileging forces infect all institutions of the social system, none are spared. Religion. Education. Sport and Leisure. The economy. Family. Government. Military. Media. Entertainment. All are infected, and all, again, 'interlock and intersect' to maintain structures of marginalization and oppression synergistically and effectively. All must be seen as mutually interdependent. In addition, the economic determinists will point out that an amoral - and hence, I argue, immoral global capitalism - works synergistically with the heads of the othering body of the Hydra.

Embracing a "Code of Ethics for Privileged Anti-Othering Persons" means understanding that one simultaneously may be privileged *and* marginalized. For example, a queer black male from the minority world, aka Global North, enjoys male and Global North privilege while enduing heteronormativity and racism. Privilege always depends upon the social context currently inhabited and changes even from moment to moment.

Humanitarian Imperative and Bending the Arc

For me, the humanitarian imperative begins with the assumption that all human lives have equal value, and every human deserves a life marked by dignity and access to basic human rights. Those who commit to humanitarian values must aggressively fight all of the systemic 'isms' represented by the heads of the Hydra. Cutting off one head is not only futile but impossible: as per the myth of the Hydra, it will only come back as two. Hence the body of the Hydra, fed by toxic othering, must be the focus of our attacks. That means a comprehensive and coordinated effort to address all systemic misuse of power certainly by individuals but even more importantly by institutions wielding power, clearly including the humanitarian sector itself. Ultimately, since human nature - albeit the darker parts - produced the Hydra, the Hydra must be tamed and transformed, not killed.

In previous posts, I have used the language and imagery of defeating the Hydra, not by lopping off each head but rather by fatally attacking the Hydra's body. Defeating the body, the toxic engine supporting and perpetuating each of the heads, seemed a logical action point. Upon reflection, I must admit that my manner of framing the solution – killing the Hydra - was perhaps yet another example of toxic masculinity emerging from my imagination. Taming rather than killing reflects perhaps a more feminist - and humane - approach. Indeed, I would have done well reading more by and about bell hooks (and others) who articulated long ago the feminist model of conflict resolution which advocates the "… deconstruction of unequal power relationships in societal structures."

Not only is taming the better goal, but it is also, looking more closely, the only way forward that pays attention to the fundamental fact that we cannot 'change human nature.' The evolutionary psychologist will tell us that how our brain works is, in large part, based on our evolutionary history and that our basic emotions are deeply wired into our brains, specifically located in the limbic system. We can't eliminate fear, a basic emotion, but we can, as President Kennedy argued, work toward a gradual evolution of human institutions.

My previous thinking was wrong, misleading, and borderline misogynistic. Taming, not killing the Hydra must be our goal.

Another shortcoming in my previous thoughts on the Hydra was too little attention to what it means to 'deconstruct unequal power relationships.' Bending the moral arc toward justice means identifying and then reversing all instances where hatred and fear have been encoded into norms, policies, and laws on all levels, locally, nationally, and internationally. This includes, of course, all the organizations and bureaucracies in which we learn and work. This work demands a close reading of [all] local, national and global history sometimes made difficult by racist resistance. The 1619 Project is a good model for a deeper examination of how racism has permeated US history.

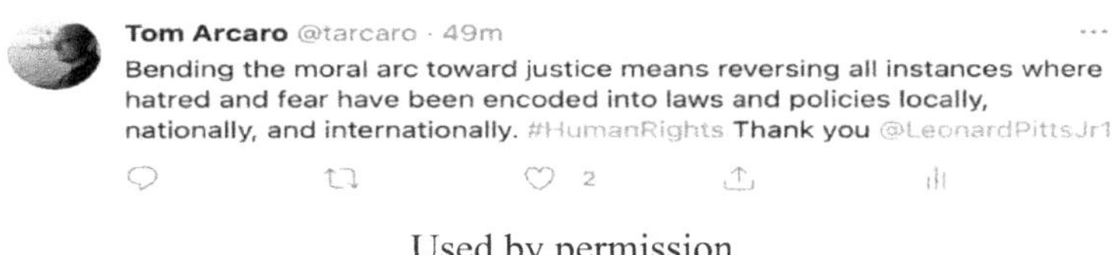

Used by permission

Though our illustration above implies otherwise, some heads of the Hydra might well be seen as far more important than others. To wit, racism impacts most of the people on this planet and thus must be confronted with a full measure of effort. That said, the fight against systemic racism needs to be anchored in rooting out power misuse allowing for all forms of toxic othering.

How can this be accomplished by an underfunded humanitarian industry designed mostly to respond to natural and human-made crises? There is no quick or easy answer to that, but I do suspect that Donini (quoted above) is right: humanitarianism is a discourse of power. One very important step in understanding and then changing toxic power arrangements is to listen to and work with those who have been marginalized by misuse of power. Those who are multiply marginalized (especially women of color) have much to teach, and it is our job to listen and to follow their lead, always demanding an inclusive scope of both understanding and action.

One such voice is NAMATI. Established five years ago, NAMATI.org is a global legal empowerment movement. From their website: "Namati means 'bending the arc.' With leadership from those most impacted, we will bend the arc of history together." The current #BlackLivesMatter movement is a vital part of bending the 'moral arc of the universe toward justice.'[1]

This phrase has a long history, with President Barack Obama borrowing it from Dr. Martin Luther King, Jr. who adapted it from abolitionist minister Theodore Parker. Parker said,

> *I do not pretend to understand the moral universe. The arc is a long one. My eye reaches but little ways. I cannot calculate the curve and complete the figure by experience of sight. I can divine it by conscience. And from what I see I am sure it bends toward justice.*

Bending this arc is a long process, and one that takes constant, coordinated effort. Gains won must be aggressively preserved or they can be lost very quickly. The NAMATI organization has it right: legal changes are key in bending the arc.

> *Before the victory is won, some more may have to face physical death, but if physical death is the price that some must pay to free their children and their white brothers from an eternal psychological death and eternal death of the spirit, then another can be more redemptive.* ***Yes, we shall overcome, because the arc of the moral universe is long, but it bends to justice.***

Quoted from Dr. Martin Luther King's I Have a Dream Speech.

Rev Dr. Martin Luther King, Jr. "I Have a Dream" speech stressed that structures within all other social institutions must be altered as well. Humanitarians have great potential and responsibility as 'arc benders' and, as stressed one more time, demands accepting leadership 'from those most impacted.'

John Lewis.
Picture from the United States House of Representatives
Wikipedia.

Understanding interconnected and baked in privileging forces and then responding to the humanitarian imperative is hard, complicated, and a long-term commitment. But is a commitment mandated by our devotion to the cause of justice for all. This mandate includes, well, inclusion, and we must act on the fact that all the heads of the Hydra are fueled by othering and hate.

In the words of the late John Lewis, champion of civil rights, we must

> *Continue to build union between movements stretching across the globe because we must put away our willingness to profit from the exploitation of others.*

The title of his posthumously published editorial is "Together, You Can Redeem the Soul of Your Nation" but I feel he would approve of this re-statement:" Together, we can redeem the soul of humanity" so that it adds a call to action for those subscribing to the "Code of Ethics for Privileged Anti-Othering Persons" discussed above. To "redeem the soul of humanity" and to bend the moral arc of the universe toward justice means confronting, challenging, and changing some near-sacred social structures. Focused social change is never quick nor easy, and we must be willing to make "good trouble" to make this happen.

A broader perspective?

Are we bending the arc? It might not seem so if you look only at the last six months or even 60 years. What if we look at the last 6000 years? According to Steven Pinker, there has been steady progress toward a more 'civilized' world. He argues in his 2011 book, *The Better Angels of Our Nature: Why Violence Has Declined*, that as a species we have become progressively less violent and cruel to others, that world cultures have slowly become more intolerant of violence in the family, and within and between peoples.

Justification for othering comes from many sources throughout history, and one section focuses on the Abrahamic religions. Pinker writes,

> *The scriptures present a God who delights in genocide, rape, slavery, and the execution of nonconformists, and for millennia those writings were used to rationalize the massacre of infidels, the ownership of women, the beating of children, dominion over animals, and the persecution of heretics and homosexuals. Humanitarian reforms such as the elimination of cruel punishment, the dissemination of empathy-inducing novels, and the abolition of slavery were met with fierce opposition in their time by ecclesiastical authorities and their apologists. The elevation of parochial values to the realm of the sacred is a license to dismiss other people's interests, and an imperative to reject the possibility of compromise.*

Concept by Tom Arcaro

The humanitarian reforms that Pinker meticulously details over many chapters are actions that bend the moral arc. They have had a cumulatively powerful impact, creating at least a less overtly violent world and at best, a more just and moral humanity.

Let's push Pinker a bit. I'll grant his historical observations, but question whether in this 21st century the pendulum may be swinging back. Is it possible that the net actions of humans in the last 20 years have undone much of this 'positive bending' of the moral arc? Have greed and gluttony been so thoroughly normalized and glorified in our global culture that even the better angels of our nature cannot purge them?

In 1940 - 80 years ago - at the very end of *The Great Dictator*, Charlie Chaplin gave an amazing and passionate speech saying that "greed has poisoned men's souls" and calling on humanity to reject those motivated by greed and who pedal fascism. According to many social critics unchecked capitalism and neoliberalism in the last 80 years have served only to further ossify toxic values serving only the ultra-rich. Though Chaplin's speech champions the resilience and morality of the human spirit, there is current evidence that fascism may have again been embraced by those in power in many parts of the world. Saudi Arabia under Mohammed bin Salam. Myanmar under Aung San Suu Kyi. Russia under Putin. Brazil under Bolsonaro. And, yes, perhaps, the United States under Donald Trump.

I'll offer that an antidote to the poison of fascism is to embrace the "Code of Ethics for Privileged Anti-Othering Persons" I presented above. Those of us, like Charlie Chaplin, who believe in the power of humanity have a moral duty to resist injustice in all forms.

Final Note

My students have suggested that the Hydra needs another head describing our species' anthropocentric perspective and the consequent destructive 'ecocidal' relationship we have with the environment. We 'other' the very natural world that sustains us and this has led us to the brink of a massive climate change which has already exacerbated humanitarian crises across the globe, mostly in the majority world. This impact is an example of environmental racism in action, and as such merits our immediate attention.

Adding 'anthropocentrism' as an additional head to the Hydra may be in order. See the chapter on "The Hydra Just Grew Yet Another Head" for more information.

[1]This section on bending the arc toward justice is an edited version of what I previously posted in other readings on my blog, "Hearing Voices" which is constantly updated.

Chapter 9
More on the Origin of the Hydra Concept

Blog post originally posted on September 25, 2020

On the Origin of the Hydra Concept

I have been teaching sections of Introduction to Sociology every semester for the last four decades. Over the years, every course text I've used has had useful chapters on 'Race and Ethnic Relations', Social Stratification', and 'Sex and Gender.' Through trial and error, I have adapted various definitions of the many 'isms', but about 20 years ago I began using this definition of racism:

Racism is an ideology of domination and subordination based on the assumption of the inherent biological and/or cultural inferiority of *other groups* and the use of this assumption to legitimize or rationalize the inferior or unequal treatment of this group.

About ten years ago I started testing my students' ability to 'connect the dots' by giving them the definition of racism and then immediately asking for a good definition of sexism, and then classism. Most picked up on the connection quickly.

Sexism is an ideology of domination and subordination based on the assumption of the inherent biological and/or cultural inferiority of *females* and the use of this assumption to legitimize or rationalize the inferior or unequal treatment of *women*.

Classism is an ideology of domination and subordination based on the assumption of the inherent biological and/or cultural inferiority of poor people and the use of this assumption to legitimize or rationalize the inferior or unequal treatment of poor people.

When I was invited to speak at the 2019 ALNAP conference about 'privileging forces' impacting how the humanitarian sector functions, I pulled an idea from an article published by Subcomandante Marcos in

Academia.Org called *"The Zapatistas and the Capitalist Hydra: Theorizing and Responding to Mexico's Crisis"* of the EZLN. Marcos once again warned about the Hydra of capitalism and the rise of virulent neoliberalism particularly in the West. I have had the honor of spending time in Zapatista territory and learning from these indigenous leaders. The EZLN movement remains strong after decades of struggle, and there are plans next spring for an EZLN party to travel to Europe to join with like-minded groups in the global and growing effort to confront toxic neoliberal ideologies.

Author sitting with the Zapatista junta
leaders in Oventic, Chiapas, MX

I asked my brother and collaborator, himself an Iraqi refugee, to draw the vision I had in my head. Our original draft of the Hydra had only five heads, but during the ALNAP conference in Berlin I soon realized more heads were called for, and the first Hydra model was redrawn to include Ableism and Ageism.

Using my original definitional frame, here are the other 'heads' or 'isms.'

Colonialism/paternalism is an ideology of domination and subordination based on the assumption of the inherent biological and/or cultural inferiority of peoples in the majority world and the use of this assumption to legitimize or rationalize the inferior or unequal treatment of these groups.

Hetero/cis-normativity is an ideology of domination and subordination based on the assumption of the inherent biological and/or cultural inferiority of non-gender comforting/queer people and the use of this assumption to legitimize or rationalize the inferior or unequal treatment of this group.

Ableism is an ideology of domination and subordination based on the assumption of the inherent biological and/or cultural inferiority of differently abled people and the use of this assumption to legitimize or rationalize the inferior or unequal treatment of this group.

Ageism is an ideology of domination and subordination based on the assumption of the inherent biological and/or cultural inferiority of older or younger people and the use of this assumption to legitimize or rationalize the inferior or unequal treatment of these groups.

All of the above definitions need expanding and deepening, of course, but taken together they can serve to underline my critical point, namely all of these 'isms' are fundamentally driven by the same process; they all begin with one group othering another and then exploiting any asymmetry of power.

Key terms in the basic definition include:

- Ideology.
- Domination and subordination.
- Assumption of biological and/or cultural inferiority.
- Legitimize and rationalize inferior or unequal treatment.

An *ideology* is sometimes explicit and obvious, but oftentimes an ideology can be an array of background ideas that, when pressed, an individual may have trouble clearly articulating. *Domination and subordination* can take many forms ranging from subtle marginalization to 'ethnic cleansing', pogroms, and genocide. *Assumptions of biological and/or cultural inferiority* are asserted by the dominant group, and this frequently leads to the dehumanization and counter anthropomorphizing of those in the 'inferior' group, and this makes any harmful actions seem *legitimate or rational.*

The Hydra metaphor seems useful, with many students frequently pointing out that 'I had never thought about how all of these social justice issues were connected.' I always ask each class of students to critique my definitions and this Hydra model, and their ideas are frequently challenging and useful. The Hydra continues to evolve.

Then 2020 Happened

Since returning from the ALNAP conference I have expanded on the Hydra concept in a series of blog posts, to be included in my forthcoming book *"Hearing Voices: Dispatches from the margins of the humanitarian sector.*

Then 2020 happened. COVID-19 put the worlds into a social, psychological, and economic downward spiral, and then George Floyd was murdered and #BlackLivesMatter took on massive, global importance.

Chapter 10
The Hydra Just Grew Another Head

Blog post originally posted April 2021

The Hydra just grew another head

Working on the Hydra concept has been a journey. I have been constantly challenged to expand and explore this image from the very beginning. What I present below is the fourth version of the Hydra, and this post continues the discussion started in Chapter 8 "A Code of Ethics for Privileged Anti-Othering Persons: The humanitarian Imperative and Hydra Revisited." As a final note I wrote:

> *My students have suggested that the Hydra needs another head describing our species' anthropocentric perspective and the consequent destructive 'ecocidal' relationship we have with the environment. We 'other' the very natural world that sustains us and this has led us to the brink of a massive climate disaster, which has already exacerbated humanitarian crises across the globe, mostly in the majority world. This impact is an example of environmental racism in action, and as such merits our immediate attention. Adding 'anthropocentrism' as an additional head to the Hydra may be in order.*

Below I discuss this new head, anthropocentrism, but I also add a comment about how unchecked capitalism and neoliberalism fuel the Hydra. If othering is the engine of all the heads, these two elements are the fuel.

Climate Change is Creating More
Work for Humanitarians

The climate crisis facing humanity is real, imminent, and will continue to cause with increasing frequency natural disasters that will necessitate response from the humanitarian sector. According to the Centers for Disease

Control (CDC), there are approximately 400 natural disasters each year, many of which are responded to by emergency relief organizations. There is ample data indicating that weather events are becoming more extreme due to climate change, and this means more events like the cyclones that hit Mozambique in 2019 and 2021.

The climate crisis chronically exasperates the perpetual blurring between aid and development work. This point is made by Seck (2007) in this Human Development Report section, *"Links Between Natural Disasters, Humanitarian Assistance and Disaster Risk Reduction: A Critical Perspective."* He states:

> *... the fact that humanitarian assistance is rooted in a shared belief that there is a moral imperative to assist people in times of stress makes it a highly reactive field. However, as a survey of World Bank task managers indicate, the best way to address the needs of the poor in natural disaster projects is to ensure that prevention and mitigation programmes are developed to guarantee that their homes did not fall down in the first place.*

He goes on further to say,

> *... risk reduction has gained prominence and is increasingly seen...as a critical component of sustainable development.*

Anthropomorphism: A New Head

The Hydra is driven by the human tendency to 'other', and all heads of the Hydra share essentially the same definition.

Anthropomorphism is an ideology of domination and subordination based on the assumption that humans are the apex species on earth and the use of this assumption to legitimize or rationalize the domination and exploitation of all life, both plant and animal.

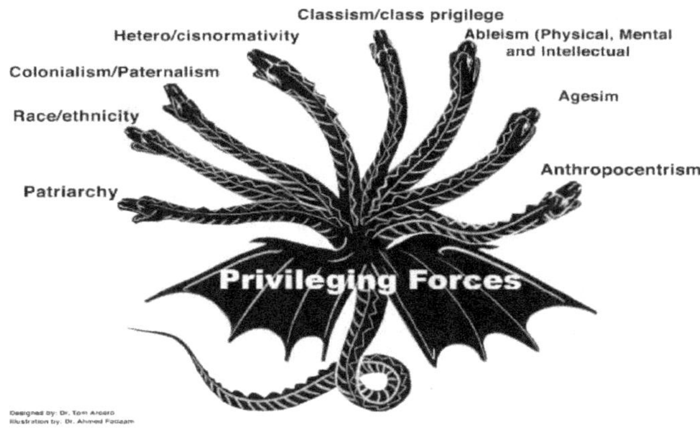

For most of our existence on the planet, humans have lived as another species, part of the ecosystem in much the same manner as all other life forms. Beginning about 12,000 years ago we began the process of domesticating animals, first sheep and goats and then dogs and cats. Soon after, about 10,000 years ago, humans began to domesticate grains, pulses, and, later, various tree varieties (e.g., olive). The purposeful genetic manipulation of plant and animal species to maximize their usefulness for humans, not coincidentally, happens about the same time we see religions getting more dominant and complex and the emergence of deities believed in and worshipped by people across the globe.

The Abrahamic religions emerged about 2000 years ago and dominated much of the world, particularly in the West and the Middle East. A look at two of these religions illustrate how anthropocentric assumptions were woven into their dogma. We are told both in the *Qur'an* and the *Holy Bible* that God created the 'heavens and the earth'. Here is Genesis 1:26,

> *Let us make man in our image, after our likeness. And **let them have dominion** over the fish of the sea and over the birds of the heavens and over the livestock and over all the earth and over every creeping thing that creeps on the earth.* (Emphasis added).

Anthropocentrism is part of what I have called the 'mentality of exploitation', a set of assumptions about our relationship with nature giving license to humans to act in a way that has now created increasing climate change, massive extinctions, and grotesque environmental degradation. Taming this head of the Hydra will mean confronting deeply entrenched theological and political/economic forces. No small task, that.

Cure the Disease *and* Treat the Symptoms

One humanitarian told me that doing his job was like 'putting a band-aid on a cancer victim', highlighting the all too true trope of the need to 'drain the swamp' as opposed to merely swatting at infinite mosquitos. In chapter 5 of *"Bringing Sandwiches to the Gates of Auschwitz,"* this is how Bernard-Henri Levy put it. As Seck argues, and I agree, the humanitarian sector must be both proactive and reactive. Though he is referring to only responses to climate change-related 'natural' disasters, I believe this is exactly the stance that we must take regarding all humanitarian responses. The rub is the age-old tension between humanitarian action and humanitarian advocacy. Humanitarian action is framed as apolitical, neutral. Humanitarian advocacy at times must be overtly political, taking sides.

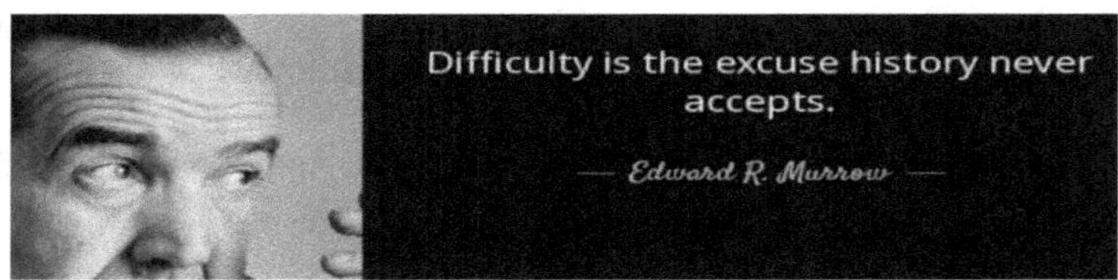

Our road ahead as 21st century humanitarians is fraught with such dilemmas, and we have no option but to dig in and openly address such issues. The words of Edward R. Murrow, an American journalist seem appropriate here. Indeed, "Difficulty is the excuse history never accepts."

How do unchecked capitalism and neoliberalism fuel the Hydra? Good questions worthy of extensive exploration in future blog posts.

Chapter 11
A Group Exercise Using the Hydra

Blog post originally posted on April 3, 2021

A Group Exercise Using the Hydra

Below is a group exercise to help deepen understanding of the Hydra's privileging forces. Before starting this exercise, you might consider the following questions:

- What does each head represent?
- Which is the oldest? Newest? Most likely to have various avatars?
- What is your score based on each being binary (1 or 0)?
- How is each demonstratively NOT binary?
- In each group of people, how many scores are possible (e.g., in a class meeting)?
- Which privileges trump others in mixed groups?
- How does the importance of each vary by social context?
- What wired-in (i.e., human nature) forces fuel the Hydra?
- What cultural forces fuel the Hydra?
- What does taming the Hydra look like?
- What 'bending the arc' changes in laws, policies, and/or behaviors related to one force help with taming other forces?
- How can we think in terms of the unit of analysis (e.g., the individual vs an organization, government, etc.) when assessing these forces and imagining ways to address them?
- What is one's 'master status' and how does this relate to privileges people (you?) have?
- How does understanding all this material about the Hydra and privileging forces help you to have a more nuanced understanding of social problems locally, nationally, and globally?

Noting Your Privilege

Though not a high percentage of our overall population, globally many people would be on the marginalized side of all eight heads of the Hydra. One can imagine for example, an elderly, poor, blind, non-white, lesbian from the majority world (aka Global South). That point granted, most people across the world 'enjoy' one or more privileges.

Identify all your privileges. One by one describe a situation where you gained some benefit or advantage from each. Now consider the following questions:

- Assuming you enjoy more than one privileged status, are there situations where you were not sure which privilege gave you an advantage in a particular situation?
- Were there situations when you realized in the moment that you were enjoying this privilege?
- Were there situations when you realized only later after reflection that you had enjoyed this privilege?
- Do you think others in the situation who shared your privilege knew you were gaining an advantage based on your privilege? How do you think they felt?
- Do you think others in the situation who did not share your privilege knew you were gaining an advantage based on your privilege? How do you think they felt?
- In each situation, how did you feel about gaining advantage based on your privilege?
- As you move through your day how common is it for you to go from a situation where you have privilege to one where you are marginalized?
- To what degree were you aware that you could use your position of privilege to be an ally to others? What does it mean to be an ally?

- Describe a situation where you simultaneously were both privileged and marginalized.

All the above questions should be answered first by everyone in writing and then shared with the group. These questions can quickly become personal, and indeed that is the point. Many will raise concerns about things like shared values, religion, and political ideology. A trusting and respectful atmosphere must be created and maintained as any discussion proceeds. A final question might be 'what have you learned about yourself, about the culture in which you live, and the larger world of other cultures across the globe.

Chapter 12
Hydra Theory 101

Blog post originally posted on April 2021
Significantly Updated April 2021

> *"My intent has been, is, and will continue to be, that those who read my works shall think and meditate upon fundamental problems, and has never been to hand them completed thoughts. I have always sought to agitate and, even better, to stimulate, rather than to instruct. Neither do I sell bread, nor is it bread, but yeast or ferment."*
> —Miguel de Unamuno

Preface

Humanitarians in all contexts need to be mindful of how privileging forces come into play in virtually every interaction, person to person or organization to organization; within one's organization or between the home organization and the affected populations. Awareness of cultural context is paramount, and understanding the Hydra is a useful tool. Standard training for any humanitarian includes defining and identifying examples of ethnocentrism. 'Ethno' means group and thus ethnocentrism is seeing everything from the value system and perspective of one's own group or culture. Just as you will be hard pressed to be an effective humanitarian being ethnocentric, the same goes for being myopically centered in other ways. Think now of the heads of the Hydra.

Probing Deeper with More Questions

The Hydra analogy can be useful, and discussions should always be grounded using practical examples that resonate on both the personal and organizational level. That said, I think there is a place for 'Hydra Theory 101.' Here are some additional thoughts and questions related to privileging forces, each a good point of departure for a deeper understanding. To be clear, all the short explanations I add to each are barely scratching the surface of what could be more deeply explored.

Racism the Most Significant Privileging Force?

Granted the basic fact of the complex and powerful intersectionality of all eight forces, each is unique. As they are depicted in the image of the Hydra, each head is the same size, inferring equivalent danger and harm. But can that be true?

Certainly, in this time of #BLM it can be argued that racism and the xenophobia it gives rise to is far more powerful than most of the other privileging forces? But what about the other forces? Which is worse, sexism of racism, and by what measures? Can ableism be put next to classism in terms of harm?

What Factors Are Involved?

Elsewhere I have argued that differentiation almost always deteriorates into stratification. Within the framework of sociocultural evolution, it is not until recently, that is about 6000 years ago, that humans began to organize themselves into non-nomadic states. Prior to that we lived in much smaller groups mostly characterized by an egalitarian way of life. With the rise of agriculture and the domestication of animals and plant materials came this new form of social organization. It is in this context that all the heads of the Hydra became much more virulent, and the transition from differentiation to stratification happened time after time. At the macro level a long view of world history indicates that many forms of differentiation resisted any such transition for tens of thousands of years, with perhaps hetero/cisnormatity and anthropocentrism being two examples.

Anthropologists describe many cultures which functioned very well rejecting the concept of gender binary and which lived with an ethos that humans are part of nature and needed to respect other life on the planet.

On a more micro level, during face-to-face interaction for example, some differences in privileging statuses can remain benign for long periods only to degenerate into toxic othering. With rare exceptions, people have some privileged statues in most social interactions relative to the others present. Indeed, one can be on both sides of the othering dynamic. The array and complexity of relative privileging statues increases exponentially as the number of participants increases. Every interaction has the possibility of being a microaggression[1], intended or, more frequently, unintended. How does the flow of interactions become impacted by harmful comments (verbal or non-verbal)?

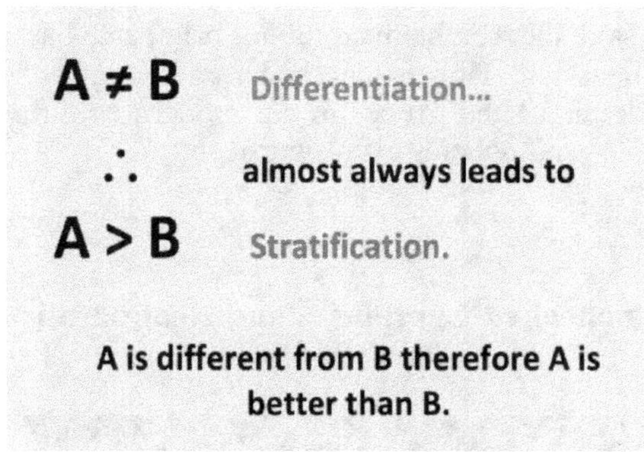

Concept by Tom Arcaro.

On both the macro and micro levels, under what circumstances are these processes accelerated? Remain inhibited? Avoided all together?

Which Are Easier to Grasp?

Are some of the privileging forces more obvious to the typical observer and hence easier to grasp than others? Do most people even accept the premise of anthropocentrism? I think it is good to ask if the groups of individuals who are likely to be marginalized have their voices heard and under what conditions. Do most people even accept the premise of anthropocentrism, for example?

Religions Normalizing and
Institutionalizing Privileging?

Are some privileging forces more deeply woven into our major religions than others, for example sexism and heteronormativity? Certainly, in their most fundamentalist forms all three Abrahamic religions appear to support racism, sexism, and heteronormativity at least as interpreted by the Taliban in Afghanistan and evangelicals in the US. Both seem quite certain that women and non-heteronormative people need to be treated as inferiors. That said, the Abrahamic religions originated based on ideologies of love and compassion. How is that the baser emotions of hatred and fear have come to dominate the fringes in our modern cultures and to impact many norms, laws, and policies even significantly?

Unchecked Capitalism and Neoliberalism
Fuel the Hydra

Picture of Tom Arcaro. Used with permission.

And now we must address the elephant in the room and ask the question, 'Are some of the forces exasperated by and/or understood more easily relative to the forces of capitalism and neoliberalism than others?' My cards on the table: I do believe that unchecked capitalism and neoliberalism have glorified and normalized gluttony and greed. We live in an absurd world where many billionaires have more money than anyone could use in hundreds of lifetimes.

Neoliberalism is an ideology based on the assumption that a free market is efficient in proportion to levels of government regulation: less control equals more freedom and efficiency. A free market, unhindered by governments or governmental regulation, will be able to organically identify and then find a way to monetize the satisfaction of all human needs. Capitalism is the economic system which drives the neoliberal agenda. Neoliberalism may indeed be the ideology that determines much of our global culture.

I have written in some detail that all the heads of the Hydra have in common the act of 'othering', and that social differentiation - any differences humans may have - almost inevitably degenerates into stratification where one group justifies dominating the other. All of the 'isms' represented by the Hydra are made possible by othering and the subsequent justification of the domination of one group by another.

If othering is the heart of the Hydra, then perhaps capitalism and neoliberalism are the food, the fuel?

Let's go through each of the eight heads of the Hydra and imagine how capitalism and neoliberalism make them more toxic, more dangerous.

- **Patriarchy:** Does capitalism support the patriarchy? Can feminism and capitalism coexist? How do patriarchy and capitalism jointly reinforce the oppression of women? (See article on patriarchy and capitalism listed in For More Information below.) These are just a few of the many questions that must be asked, and there are scores of scholars, past and present, doing just that, most answering with a strong affirmation that capitalism contributes to sexism.
- **Racism:** Some argue that racism and capitalism are conjoined twins. The North Atlantic slave trade is just one example; there are countless others. This is worth extensive discussion and is indeed the premise of countless books and articles.
- **Colonialism/Paternalism:** A recent article in *The Guardian* "The Invention of Whiteness: The Long History of a Dangerous Idea" (listed in For More Information) does a very good job sketching out how 'whiteness' was invented and then used to justify racism and its place in the rise of the colonial powers. William Easterly's *The Tyranny of Experts* (see chapter 4) is an earlier description of the

same. The research on this topic is copious, compelling, and a must read for anyone wanting to 'decolonize' the humanitarian sector.

- **Hetero/cisnormativity**: The argument that "Queer Oppression Is Etched in the Heart of Capitalism" (listed in For More Information) is not uncontroversial, and there is a rich (albeit somewhat recent) range of discussion on this topic.
- **Classism/class privilege:** Well, this one speaks for itself. Charles Darwin and Karl Marx had much in common but nothing more significant than the fact that they both articulated fundamental algorithms. Biologist Theodosius Dobzhansky argued that "Nothing in Biology Makes Sense Except in the Light of Evolution" (listed in For More Information section). In that same vein and following the lead of the economic determinism articulated by Marx, I will argue that nothing in society makes sense except in the light of capitalism. This, of course, includes all the damage done by the glorification and normalization of gluttony and greed.
- **Ableism (physical, mental, and intellectual):** As I write this there are waves of critique aimed at the United States for hoarding vaccines. Disasters - in this case a global pandemic - always hit those on the margins the hardest, especially physical or health related events. That COVID has been horrific for those who are disabled is not in question. Capitalism is based on a myopic quest to maximize profits, and hence have both an economic and ideological interest to exclude workers based on perceived disability.
- **Ageism:** Linked to ableism, ageism is woven into the very fabric of modern capitalism where workforces value youth. Capitalism profits from making us fear aging.
- **Anthropocentrism:** We are on the brink of environmental collapse. The climate crisis is real and is causing increasingly frequent extreme weather events which generate the need for a humanitarian response. The US lead April 2021 Zoom meeting of global leaders yielded more talk than action largely because the mantra of capitalism is to protect jobs at any cost. Our mentality of exploitation is driven by our quest for 'freedom' from oppressive government interference, the very core philosophy of liberalism. Destruction of the planet will proceed apace if there's a buck to be made. Convince me otherwise.

Each of the above discussions is worth having in greater detail, of course, but I think my point has been made: the heads of the Hydra are all fueled by capitalism and neoliberal ideas.

Adding to the 'white savior' trope

Teju Cole helped to popularize the 'white savior' trope with his now canonical 2012 article aggressively and appropriately titled *"The White-Savior Industrial Complex,* and now one can find countless uses of the 'white savior' idea in both academic and popular culture discussions. So, if there is a white savior complex, can there be a 'male savior complex'?

As we inventory all eight heads of the Hydra coming up with parallel 'savior complexes' is both useful and instructive.

The 'white savior' obviously comes into play when examining both racism and colonialism/paternalism. As mentioned above, the 'male savior' complex is one manifestation of sexism and patriarchy. Perhaps slightly harder to articulate is 'hetero/cis saviorism' where 'normal' persons try to save queer people from their 'deviant' behavior. 'Class saviorism' can be seen in many guises, perhaps the most obvious of which is 'charity' for the poor. 'Able saviorism' is complicated because of the various dimensions of ableism, namely physical, mental, and intellectual. Able person's frequently want to 'help' those differently abled and do at times in grotesquely patronizing ways. 'Young saviors' are quick to make assumptions about older people and want to 'help' them. The final head of the Hydra, anthropocentrism, in hoary campaigns like 'save the whales' and 'save Mother Earth.'

Each savior complex touched on above deserves its own lengthy discussion. What these savior complexes all have in common is that each in their own way belittles and robs dignity from the group being 'saved.' When you' other' it makes you feel superior, allowing for marginalizing interactions. These interactions, oft times overtly patronizing, serve to affirm the superior/inferior relationship but done so in such a way that it 'feels good' as in 'we're helping the poor starving children in Africa' for example.

Just as there are numerous articles which unpack white saviorism there are articles, I am certain, which unpack all the other 'saviorism's' as well. The utility of the Hydra metaphor is that it facilitates seeing all these patronizing forces as different manifestations of the same process. When you unpack one you unpack them all.

Additional Questions to Consider:

- With respect to intersectionality, are some forces more salient than others, i.e., have more multiplicative properties?
- Are some of these forces more culturally universal than others? Indeed, as our world becomes more globalized and homogenized by transnational trade, communication, and media consumption I will argue that toxic privileging forces exist in varying degrees in all world cultures.
- People can have privileged statuses, of course, but so can organizations. Does an INGO based in the Global North have more sway in, for example, a cluster meeting?
- By taming these individual heads, I mean 'bending the moral arc' by changing behavioral norms, instituting policies, passing and enforcing local, national, and international laws, and other proactive measures. Which heads are easiest to tame, and which are the hardest? Related, do (for example) passing laws related to one head make change relative to the other heads easier? Do anti-sexism laws impact laws related to racism or vice versa, for example?

Hydra Theory 101

I started this post with a quote from my favorite philosopher, Miguel de Unamuno. He said, *"Neither do I sell bread, nor is it bread, but yeast or ferment."* And that is exactly what I am offering here, an invitation to press to its edges this Hydra metaphor. From these abstract ideas and challenges, I suggest we now turn to something more straightforward.

A Group Exercise Using the Hydra

Below is a group exercise which may help individuals deepen understanding of the Hydra's privileging forces. This exercise can be used with everyone from young undergraduates to seasoned humanitarians. A facilitator will need to frame the exercise and act as a guide through the questions and subsequent discussion, taking notes as examples are given and points are made.

Noting Your Privilege: An Exercise

Though not a high percentage of our overall population, globally there are many people who would be on the marginalized side of all seven (now eight counting anthropocentrism) heads of the Hydra. One can imagine, for example, an elderly, poor, blind, non-white, lesbian from the majority world (aka Global South). That point granted, the vast majority of people across the world 'enjoy' one or more privileged statues.

For this exercise identity all your privileges. One by one describe a situation where you gained some benefit or advantage from each. Now consider the following questions: Assuming you enjoy more than one privileged status, are there situations where you were not sure which privilege gave you an advantage in a particular situation?

- Were there situations when you realized in the moment that you were enjoying this privilege? Were there situations when you realized only later after reflection that you had enjoyed this privilege?

- Do you think others in the situation who shared your privilege knew you were gaining advantage based on your privilege? How do you think they felt?
- Do you think others in the situation who did not share your privilege knew you were gaining advantage based on your privilege? How do you think they felt?
- In each situation, how did you feel about gaining advantages based on your privilege?
- As you move through your day how common is it for you to go from a situation where you have privilege to one where you are marginalized?
- To what degree were you aware that you could use your position of privilege to be an ally to others? What does it mean to be an ally?
- Describe a situation where you simultaneously were both privileged and marginalized.
- What norm changes, new or revised policies, laws, and/or additional enforcement of any existing or new policies and laws can you suggest that might defuse awkward, unfair, and/or marginalizing privileging asymmetries?

The facilitator can bring the discussion to a close by listing all the major points made, highlighting particularly useful and relevant examples, and by underscoring the need to examine useful, practical, and effective ways to encourage interactional patterns which minimizes the impact of these privileging forces and maximizes the chance for structural changes which mitigate the perpetuation of the negative impacts of these forces.

---

[1]Microaggressions in Everyday Life (2nd edition 2020) by Derald Wing Sue and Lisa Spanierman explore micro-aggressions in the context of higher education in the US. Their insights are easily transferred to other settings, and I think this book might be useful for those in the humanitarian sector.

Chapter 13
Taming the Hydra during the
2020 Tokyo Olympics

Blog post originally posted August 5, 2021

> [Research help for this post was provided by Elon students
> Amelia Arcaro-Burbridge and Trevor Molin]

Shining the light on positive examples

My last several blog posts [chapters] have illustrated the nature of the Hydra and have painted a dismal picture of oppressive privileging forces imposing their will on many types of marginalized groups across the globe and back through time.

Through the millennia there has been a constant tug of war between those who are driven by hate, greed, and gluttony and those who act motivated by love, compassion, and humility. The 'moral arc of the universe' may indeed bend toward justice, but for every positive movement there are negative counter actions, the former barely winning the battle over the long term. Recognizing positive actions - making them part of the news cycle - is a necessary step we need to support first to give ourselves hope, but perhaps more importantly by shining a light on these positives actions we are providing positive examples for those who want to join the cause of furthering our move toward a humanity that creates and nurtures pathways to dignity for all humans.

This exercise in identifying examples of 'taming the Hydra' reinforces the key premise that all eight heads of the Hydra are always present, and all are interconnected by various forms of toxic othering.

Taming the Hydra during the Olympics

Taming the Hydra can take many forms and is being done day by day everywhere across the globe. The <u>Olympic Games</u> bring together athletes, officials, fans, and the press from every continent and from most of our 206 nations. These games bring together different cultures, and hence many varied norms, traditions. As such provide a setting where ideas about how humans should treat other humans are out on the stage. A positive consequence of this cultural mixture is that one culture's norms, policies, and laws which are seen as oppressive are called out by those from cultures or nations who are more progressive. Olympic tradition is that all cultures should be respected, but that respect can be situationally withdrawn when universal human rights are violated. The discussion over the line between what is a cultural norm that should be respected and one which is a legitimate violation of human rights is ongoing, vigorous, and has constant political overtones. Asking hard questions is at the very core of understanding and taming the Hydra. The hard questions raised at the games are critical and illuminating.

With that spirit in mind, below are some examples of actions taken during the 2020 Tokyo Olympic games. Included are actions taken by individuals, organizations, and allies.

As with all social change efforts, there are competing forces; efforts to tame the Hydra are simultaneously being counteracted by those intended to maintain the status quo or reinforced. We have thus included examples of those individuals and organizations who act in such a way as to stifle positive social change.worse to feed the Hydra poison so that toxic othering.

Our reading of these Olympics is that this tug of war between taming and feeding is being won by those who stand for social justice and our evidence; the Hydra is being tamed, act by heroic act, in real time. We invite you to click on each hyperlink to read in more detail. Keep in mind that the Hydra is inherently intersectional, and some actions may address more than one head of the Hydra.

Please note that by including any of the hyperlinks below I am not endorsing that news outlet, nor all the points made in the article.

Please join me

The list of articles below is far from complete, and I would love to update and make it more thorough. I invite everyone who reads this post to send to me via email (arcaro@elon.edu) any additional links which illustrate actions of individuals or organizations addressing the various heads of the Hydra.

Patriarchy -fighting sexism

- U.S. Olympic Fencer, Accused of Sexual Misconduct, Kept Apart From Team   Norwegian women's beach handball team fined for not playing in bikinis
- Pink offers to pay bikini bottoms fine for Norway women's handball team
- Wearing unitards, German gymnasts promote comfort, take stand against sexualization

Race/ethnicity – confronting racial, ethnic, and religious based marginalization

- Olympic Pressure And How Black Athletes Balance Being Applauded Yet Feared
- The Olympics Rely On, but Don't Support, Black Girl Magic
- Race Imboden: What US Olympic fencer's black X symbol on his hand means
- Costa Rica's Luciana Alvarado raises fist during gymnastics floor routine in support of Black Lives Matter
- Belarusian sprinter reaches Poland after defying order home

Colonialism/Paternalism insuring representation from all peoples

- IOC Refugee Olympic Team Tokyo 2020
- Why is there a Refugee Olympic Team?

Hetero/cisnormativity – gender and sexuality inclusivity

- First openly transgender Olympians are competing in Tokyo
- There may be more Olympians who identify as LGBTQ than ever before. But there are limits to inclusion
- Record Number of LGBTQ Athletes Set to Compete at the Tokyo Olympics

Classism/class privilege

- Sha'Carri Richardson, a Track Sensation, Tests Positive for Marijuana
- How many sports are in the 2021 Tokyo Olympics? Which are the new ones?
- An unsavory history of the Olympic Games in five outfits

Ableism (Physical, Mental, and Intellectual)

- 'OK not to be OK': Mental health takes top role at Olympics
- The Paralympic Games

Ageism

- Fmr. Olympic gymnast breaks retirement, challenges ageism in pro-sports

Anthropocentrism – questioning human centered actions

- Even With Cardboard Beds And Recycled Medals, Olympics Take Flak Over The Environment
- Tokyo Olympics Medals Were Made With Tons of Recycled Smartphones, Laptops Donated by the Public

There are so many more articles to include and there will be updates made to this post.

Woke Olympics?

The Olympic games provide an amazing spotlight on cultural differences - and similarities. It is no surprise that in this #MeToo, #BLM, #Decolonize world, these Olympics would generate attention on issues about the privileging forces represented by the heads of the Hydra. We can learn much about our species and its increasingly globalized culture by observing what is written and broadcast before, during, and after the games. In a very disparaging fashion American comedian and 'commentator' Bill Maher described these as the 'woke Olympics'. I agree with him that these Olympics are calling out privileging forces that exist around the world in every institution, including sports, but rather than disparaging these efforts I respect and encourage this critical reflection on the human condition. I think applying <u>critical Hydra heory</u> can help us understand more deeply all the links above.

Chapter 14
Bringing the Hydra to class

Blog post posted on: July 5, 2021

Student reactions to the Hydra

I have been using my Hydra posts as a teaching tooling since the fall of 2019. Every semester I'll explain the idea in class and then have my students read about the Hydra, using it in some manner to help deepen their understanding of core course concepts like colonialism, racism, classism, and sexism. To the present, I have used this model in over a dozen classes, and each time my students push me to expand my thinking and to reconsider and deepen aspects of the Hydra's impact. I owe a massive debt to all my students these last several semesters.

This summer I taught online '*Sociology Through Film*' and was blessed with many very good students who, as a group, embraced the Hydra concept quickly and enthusiastically. Below you'll read what several students had to say when I proposed they find and discuss a film that addressed one or more of the Hydra heads. I was impressed by the variety of the films on which they chose to focus and, in general, how well they used some of our course content.

Many thanks to student Trinity Black for editing these essays for clarity and content.

The Hydra in Film
Elon University
Summer I 2021: SOC131 Sociology in Film

Introductory Statement
By *Caroline Borio*

As a part of Dr. Arcaro's *Sociology Through Film* course, my classmates and I were tasked with reading and understanding Dr.

Arcaro's blog posts on The Hydra metaphor and applying that knowledge to film analysis.

From the first-class discussion after we read Dr. Arcaro's blog posts, it was clear that the entire class quickly embraced the idea and was able to apply it to film analysis, and to both historical and recent events in the world around us. In that first discussion, I recall hearing my classmates explain how forces such as racism and sexism clearly intersect, and all of us at once understood why it is important to fight against not just one, but all these forces since they all stem from the same source of "othering". It was clear from the beginning that the Hydra is an incredibly useful tool for students when trying to understand privilege, and the intersectionality of these privileging forces in the world.

In the following chapter, you will see the writing some of us completed when we applied the Hydra to our study of *Sociology Through Film*. Each of us chose one of the eight heads of the Hydra on which to focus and found a film that centered around that particular privileging force. After watching the film and identifying the significance of the privileging force within the film, we were asked to write a blog post that applied the idea of the Hydra to our film. This blog post was to consist of a summary of the Hydra metaphor, a description of our chosen privileging force, and how our selected movie sheds light on that privileging force. I had the privilege of reading my classmates' blog posts, and every one of them provided a clear depiction of how their movie explored their privileging force, and why this was significant to the film's overall purpose. Through our blog posts, I recognized how the Hydra concept can be a useful tool towards recognizing privilege, intersectionality, and how we can approach the fight against these forces to create a more equitable and just society.

"Victoria and Abdul" (Colonialism/Paternalism)
By *Grant Michael*

The privileging force I'm examining is colonialism/paternalism and the movie I chose to tie into it is Victoria and Abdul. This movie focuses on the head of the British monarchy in the late 1800s, Queen Victoria, and her friendship with a common Indian man named Abdul. Through this lens, we get to see a lot of the power struggles between the queen and her subordinates, and the view on the larger colonized British Empire. Colonialism is "the practice by which a powerful country controls another country or other countries." (Colonialism) I would like to add that other definitions usually also include "to exploit its resources." Paternalism is "a system under which an authority undertakes to supply needs or regulate the conduct of those under its control in matters affecting them as individuals as well as in their relations to authority and each other." (Paternalism) This means the people in power tell those under their power what's in their best interest, with an almost "we-know-better" mentality. This movie, while on the surface seems to be about the relationship between Queen Victoria and Abdul, gives a good glimpse into the mindset and power struggles of these privileging forces.

In the movie, we see Queen Victoria in her last year of rule. The movie portrayed her well as someone who loved to rule, but at the same time knew very little about the world outside of her royal life. All the high-class members of British society we meet know very little about India but speak of it and its people as lesser compared to them. The queen, despite being its ruler, hadn't ever been there. They all have this idea that they know better than the people they rule, however they're highly unqualified to tell Indians how to live their lives halfway across the globe.

The most enlightening part for me was how everyone had made judgments about the Indians long before ever meeting someone from that part of the world. He is called "the Hindu", even know he is Muslim. He also must teach the Queen "Indian," despite there being thousands of languages and dialects spoken in India. The queen knew next to nothing about India or its culture, and it was honestly very surprising to see someone like the Queen taking on a commoner from India and learning from him, since it doesn't fit the monarchy's image. I think it was a good lesson; however, the paternalistic attitudes of the rest of the British stopped them from seeing Abdul as someone who could add any value to their lives.

I'm sure most of the rest of the British empire felt this way, too. In my opinion even now, there is a feeling of personal superiority the British hold over others. This was only one country in an empire that ruled over 58 countries, so imagine how little the queen could have known about any of the rest she ruled. These discriminatory forces are what many empires are built from.

After watching the movie, I sat down to write this blog entry, and took notice of the other heads of the Hydra I saw. I could find an example of almost every privileging force in the film. This idea that all these forces exist alongside each other means you can't just kill one head on the Hydra, you must kill them all to truly defeat it. The force of colonialism can seem far above us as individuals, but it's up to us to see the flaws within these systems and advocate against them. I think paternalism appears very prominently in the movie, and it can remind us not to make choices for people who are in groups we aren't, as Abdul knew things about the world the others barely comprehend.

"My Beautiful Laundrette" (Hetero/Cis-normativity)
By *Trinity Black*

The Hydra metaphor is a way of understanding all the privileging forces at play in our society and how they're all interconnected and rooted in the same source, like the many heads on the Hydra. Although they can't be separated from each other, the privileging forces affect people in different ways, so it's still meaningful to talk about them as separate issues.

My *Beautiful Laundrette* is an interesting film, which ends up feeling more like you're watching a short section of someone's life unfold instead of a movie. "The movie is not concerned with plot, but with giving us a feeling for the society its characters inhabit. Modern Britain is a study in contrasts, between rich and poor, between upper and lower classes, between native British and the various immigrant groups– some of which, such as the Pakistanis, have started to prosper. To this mixture, the movie adds the conflict between straight and gay." (Ebert) The contrasts in the movie make it interesting to look at through the perspective of the Hydra, with every character being marginalized but also benefiting from a privileging force in some way. A lot is going on in the film which isn't relevant to hetero/cis-normativity, so I highly recommend watching it to get a better feel of how many other heads of the Hydra it depicts and their intersectionality.

Honestly, cis-normativity isn't very present in the film, at least not in a way that's meaningful to discuss. There's a lack of transgender representation, but that means there isn't anything to talk about concerning its depiction of cissexism, besides the fact that you are meant to assume all the characters are cis. There's a one-off comment about Omar's penis by his father, and then nothing else. However, heteronormativity is much more visible.

In the entire first third or so of the movie, there are a few hints towards Omar's non-heterosexuality, but mostly we see characters unquestioningly uphold heteronormativity. Near the beginning, Omar's father remarks to his brother Nasser over the phone that he should see about finding Omar a wife while getting him a job, implying he's about the age where it's expected, but hasn't taken any significant interest in women. Later, when Omar visits Nasser's house, he reconnects with his cousin Tania and she makes sexual/romantic advances to him, which he responds to. There are also points where Nasser and Tania herself suggest her as a marriage prospect for Omar. Even Omar's relationship with his poor white partner who rekindles a romance with him, Johnny, just comes across as reconnecting friends at first. Then, about 44 minutes into the film, it's made clear that Omar and Johnny are involved with each other when they kiss in an alley.

Tania, Omar, and Johnny are all part of a younger generation, and they approach heterosexuality with a more casual attitude compared to the older characters. Omar and Tania casually get engaged or at least say they'll get married a few times in the film, but it's also made clear to the viewer that Omar is with Johnny and Tania wants to move out and live away from home. Both Omar and Johnny kiss Tania at a point in the film, and there's a moment where Tania is vaguely possessive over Omar, but none of these moments are played with any lasting seriousness. The possessive scene with Tania came across as humorous to me because it's quite literally the only time any character clocks them as not straight and it happens a few minutes before their kiss confirms the relationship. She realizes it because of one small, intimate (though still platonic) moment, but when Omar's uncle walks in on them half-naked later in the film, he doesn't even seem very suspicious.

All other characters in the film, including the older upper-class Pakistani characters and Johnny's old white fascist gang, seem to have no clue they're anything but heterosexual. This implies that the more conservative-minded people probably aren't even used to considering options besides heterosexuality, or at least that the people around Johnny and Omar hold such rigid views of them that they can't fit them not being straight into that view. Both their main social groups are marginalized in a way, but also benefit from a privileging force, and so heteronormativity is assumed so intensely that they barely must hide their relationship. The fact that they do hide it anyway means we know there would be consequences if they're found out.

"Joker" (Classism)
By *Harish Prasad*

All the heads of the Hydra show the types of privilege that exist around the world, with each head representing a different one. This post is about class privilege/classism head of the Hydra. It represents the conflict between upper and lower classes, and people of higher classes are assumed to be the privileged group. For instance, outside of the one percent in the US, would be the caste system in India. At the top are Brahmins, and at the bottom are the Untouchables, and most people who aren't Brahmins are looked down upon. This post will focus on the movie Joker, which depicts a conflict between the upper and lower classes well. This movie could also depict the ableism head of the Hydra, since this is a movie about a mentally ill man who is mistreated.

Joker is an origin story that centers around the Joker, Arthur Fleck, a man with a severe mental illness who lives in poverty in a beaten-down apartment. The way society treats him drives him into madness which ultimately ends in him donning his villainous alter ego as the Joker. Arthur is clearly alienated from people, even other poor people, and is thought of as a "freak" to the point where he gets fired from his job at a clown agency. This had been the case his whole life, as he lacked a social group, or a group that "consists of two or more people who regularly interact based on mutual expectations and who share a common identity." (S: UCSW, 6.1) This movie also has messages about capitalism. It can be seen as a critique of capitalism in multiple ways, but one good example in the movie is when Arthur can no longer get his medications or see his social worker anymore because they cut funding and shut down the place he goes to.

There are a few scenes that piece together the story and how this movie ties into the classism head of the Hydra. The first scene is a scene on the subway where three well-dressed guys, presumably more upper-class, harass and assault Arthur because of his brain condition that makes him unable to control his laughter at times. Arthur has a gun on him, and he kills them, which leads to something like a social movement where lower-class people start protesting.

This leads into the next scene, where Thomas Wayne talks about the murders on TV and says a couple of things that drive the point. He stands up for the men who were murdered, who were apparently Wayne Enterprises employees, and talks about what good people they were. He also talks down to the protesters for taking the side of the killer and says the murderer was clearly envious of people better off than him. At the end of the interview, Wayne says that until poor people change for the better, "those of us who made something of our lives, we'll always look at those who haven't as nothing but clowns." He also says people need to realize that he's their only hope, which is why he's running for mayor.

This leads into the last scene, which is the climax near the end of the movie, after Arthur fully transforms into the Joker. When he is on the Murray Franklin show, the Joker reveals that he's the one who killed the men on the subway. He says that he didn't kill them to start a movement; he did it because they are awful, and people are awful. He says this because almost everyone in his life mistreated him, and the system (which he criticized) left people like him to fend for themselves with no help.

The most important part of this scene is when he rolls his eyes and asks "Why is everyone so upset about these guys? If it was me dying on the sidewalk, you'd walk right over me. I pass you every day on the sidewalks and you don't notice me. And what, everyone cares about these three guys because Thomas Wayne cried about them on TV?"

Thomas Wayne being a rich guy drew all the attention to these guys, but Arthur says if the murder happened to "anyone like him" (poor and mentally ill), nobody would bat an eye, which has a lot of truth, based on the events of his tragic life. He then asks if Thomas Wayne had ever imagined what it was like to be someone like him, and says Wayne thinks that "we'll sit here, and take it like good little boys," which seemingly is the mindset of the rich in Gotham. These were the most impactful examples of how this head of the Hydra is tackled in this film (with definitely more in there

"Forrest Gump" (Ableism)
By *Hannah Ellowitz*

The Hydra metaphor proves that to fight for "all humanity," we must attack many individual yet interconnected systems from the root (or body of the creature) to break down the systems that favor certain types of people. The privileging force of ableism is a newer addition to the Hydra, and the term is defined by The Center of Disability Rights, Inc. as "a set of beliefs or practices that devalue and discriminate against people with physical, intellectual, or psychiatric disabilities and often rests on the assumption that disabled people need to be 'fixed' in one form or the other." (CDR) Leah Smith, a writer, communications professional, and disability advocate says that "Ableism is intertwined in our culture, due to many limiting beliefs about what disability does or does not mean, how able-bodied people learn to treat people with disabilities and how we are often not included at the table for key decisions."

In July 2016, the Ruderman Family Foundation (RFF) released their White Paper "On Employment of Actors with Disabilities in Television", sharing that "95 percent of characters with disabilities on television were played by able-bodied actors." (RFF) Furthermore, if the current Academy Awards trend continues as is, any actor nominated for their portrayal of a disabled/non-neuro-typical role has a 50 percent chance of winning that prestigious award.

Most notable examples include Dustin Hoffman in *Rain Man*, Eddie Redmayne in *The Theory of Everything*, and Tom Hanks in *Forrest Gump*. In the Oscar's nearly 93-year history, only two disabled actors have received awards for their work; Harold Russel was a handless non-professional actor who won Best Supporting Actor in 1946 for his role in *The Best Years of Our Lives,* and deaf actress Marlee Matlin won Best Actress title in 1986 for her portrayal of Sarah Norman in *Children of a Lesser God.*

I'm curious as to what abled viewers are so fascinated by when it comes to disabled persons in film, and how close these portrayals by able-bodied and neuro-typical actors are to the lived experiences of disabled people. I decided to watch *Forrest Gump* through a more specific lens to help me better understand ableism and its Hydra head.

Forrest Gump is iconic for its humor, charm, and heartbreak. The notoriety surrounding the story's many disabled characters brought newfound attention to the disabled community through film. The story was written, developed, and performed entirely by neuro-typical, able-bodied people. I don't at all believe that the Forrest Gump story is primarily about disability, but it is a central part of multiple main characters' livelihood, making disability a relevant piece of the story. The Amazon Prime blurb about the film describes Forrest as being slow-witted, but it's hinted throughout the film that he is disabled, despite the many wild experiences and accomplishments he achieves throughout his lifetime. The only disability that is specified in the script is that Forrest's IQ is 75. The lack of specification with Forrest's disabilities leaves audiences to stereotype his conglomeration of malfunctions into something misinformed and ableist.

The beginning of the film features a young, severely weak, and crippled Forrest running so fast that he breaks his leg braces and escapes his bullies, finally free from being physically disabled. After breaking through these physical barriers, he eventually gets accepted to a top university with a football scholarship, so "thankfully" he wouldn't need the intellectual factor to influence an acceptance.

From early on, we're shown that for a disabled person to become successful, they must rid themselves of their hindrance and become able in a way they naturally aren't. There's an excellent review question at the end of Chapter four in our text that made me question my perspective on what it means to be equal in the case of ability. "Do you agree that effective socialization is necessary for an individual to be fully human? Could this assumption imply that children with severe developmental disabilities, who cannot undergo effective socialization, are not fully human?" (S: UCSW, 4.1) Socialization is, in a way, what shapes a person into a kind of individual, but what about those who can't socialize? Forrest is incredibly social despite his disability, but how would audiences have viewed an antisocial achiever? Would it have made it as exciting of a movie?

Much of what I read by disabled bloggers and writers spoke to the character Lieutenant Dan and how they felt connected to him in more ways than they had with Forrest. Dan is presented to us as a dashing, masculine hero who Forrest is afraid to disappoint, only to have his heroism stripped when he becomes an amputee in Vietnam. The script does an okay job with allowing Dan to express his anger however he chooses, allowing him to speak directly to the overwhelmingly angry feelings experienced by many disabled viewers. Over time, Dan and Forrest develop a sort of Mice and Men dynamic, and they connect during the moment when they bring two sex workers back to their apartment after a night of drinking. After Forrest makes it clear he doesn't have any interest in the women, Dan falls out of his wheelchair in protest, leading to the women snickering and insulting them as they leave. Here, the audience is reminded what it means to be diminished, to being "crippled" or an "idiot". I think that scene brings audiences into a vulnerable moment for these characters and shows how painful it can be for disabled people to be othered. Eventually, however, Dan is "redeemed" through the gift of prosthetic legs, meaning he's now successful at acting like an abled person, free from his disability.

I don't think there was any agenda by the creators of the film to make a strong statement about disabled people– but I'd say there is a subtle commentary on the traumatic aftermath of Vietnam veterans who've developed disabilities and PTSD after their time overseas. I think there should have been more awareness and inclusion of disabled actors or creators through the development of the film, in an effort to make the story a bit more truthful to real experiences, despite the story itself being a bit satirical and humorous.

Looking at this now, almost 30 years later, it seems rather bold for able-bodied and neuro-typical people to produce a movie like *Forrest Gump*. It does seem as though folks in disabled communities resonated more with parts of this story and the effect it shows of society's othering through ableism. As we strive for a more inclusive community, I think it's most important for storytellers and creatives to consider how those receiving the stories feel about their portrayal and how the effects of viewing can help others better understand new perspectives of the human experience.

I'll end with a section of an article by Kristen Lopez on her connection to Lieutenant Dan in *Forrest Gump*:

"And yet for all the ways Lieutenant Dan is indicative of the lack of change in representation, he'll always be my first; the first time I saw someone in a wheelchair who said a lot of the things I was feeling internally regarding my disability. Outside of the story, it was amazing just to see a wheelchair on-screen. Sure, Dan uses a

standard hospital wheelchair that would provide no comfort or support for his body, let alone be difficult to wheel full-time. (No wonder he fell down ramps and almost got hit by cars!) It was obvious no one was actually disabled on the writing team, but for a child who'd only been using a wheelchair for a few years, something was better than nothing." (K. Lopez, Forbes).

"Up" (Ageism)
By *Olivia Pierce*

Tom Arcaro uses the Hydra as a metaphor to depict and frame the norms related to the privileging/oppressive forces that are fueled by "othering," the justification of one group dominating another. One of the privileging forces in Arcaro's Hydra model is ageism or discriminating against someone because of their age. Ageism assumes that the very old or the very young are biologically or culturally inferior to others. It's related to ableism, which assumes that non-abled people are inferior.

Since the very old and very young are generally assumed to be not as capable as an adult, they're linked. Ideas about their inferiority are used to justify the unequal treatment of people in these groups.

The movie *Up* highlights ageism as it relates to an elderly man, Carl Fredricksen. At the beginning of the movie, Carl is depicted as a stubborn, grumpy old man who is resistant to change and wants to be left alone. He uses a walker, has hearing aids, and wears dentures. We see examples of ageism throughout the movie, including the Wilderness Explorers' assumption that older people need assistance and have a requirement to earn a merit badge for "Assisting the Elderly."

Carl is also shown as out of touch with what's going on in the world (not knowing what a GPS is), and he's described as smelling like "prunes and denture cream." Each of the examples illustrates different dimensions of aging, as described by gerontologists: chronological, as Carl is 78 years old; biological, with his bad back, hearing impairment, dentures; psychological, by being stubborn and grumpy after losing his wife; and social, how he's seen by others. (S: UCSW, 12.1) Strictly speaking, social aging refers to the "changes in people's roles and relationships in a society as they age." (S: UCSW, 12.3).

The movie may have helped people think about their views on aging, at least temporarily. It brought out the ageism in reviewers and toy manufacturers. They had negative views about its success because "the main character, a grumpy old man, is not considered commercially attractive." (Walker) These people were essentially saying the movie did not have value because they could not profit off an elderly character.

Two studies, conducted by Humana and USC Annenberg, assessed the portrayal of older people in film and found that "few characters aged 60 and over are represented in film, and that prominent senior characters face demeaning or ageist references." They also found that those depictions were not realistic. "Our popular cultural narratives do not present the stories and experiences of seniors. As a result, viewers miss out on rich depictions that can confront our stereotypes about older individuals and broaden our views about what it means to age today." (Smith et al.)

It is interesting to note that in *Up*, Carl changes from a grumpy, stubborn man to a hero. He defies his age, fighting off the villain (although the movie sticks with elderly stereotypes by having his back go out and his dentures fall out), and ending with a new outlook on life. His determination flies in the face of ageism. It's too bad that there aren't many older characters in children's movies. It would be a great place to start changing people's views on age.

"Okja" (Anthropocentrism)
By *William Thomas*

All the heads of the Hydra can represent forces that derive from "othering" and are embedded into our culture. Each head has its own oppressive force for each way to differentiate a person from another group. The Hydra is one creature just as each head of discrimination has an interconnected relationship with the others.

Anthropocentrism is the mindset that humans are at the center of the world. This view that humans are the most important form of life appears in many aspects throughout our history and particularly Western culture. The most common example of anthropocentrism is animals vs. humans. Many will argue that a human would not be classified as an animal because of our heightened awareness and consciousness compared to the other species. However, humans are still driven by biological desires and our animal nature could be one of the driving forces of deviancy. We are creatures affected by many things, but we are also still animals and driven by biological forces. The practice of sociology argues that culture has a deeper influence on human behavior compared to biology. (S:UCSW, 3.1) This may be true, but biological forces are the initial arbiter of our actions, and our cultural influences filter out decisions that may be considered deviant.

Along with the other heads of the Hydra, anthropocentrism spreads the idea that one individual or group is superior to another. This view of the world spreads the idea to other cases. The validation of anthropocentrism validates the thought that other heads of the Hydra are acceptable ideals. The symbolism of the Hydra helps one understand that the forces of "otherism" are the same: different minds but one body.

Humans generally don't give too much attention to the suffering of animals, whether it's human-caused or some other preventable occurrence. We are willing to sacrifice animals for the greater good of humanity or individuals, even if it means killing a few elephants for a nice set of piano keys.

This draws back into our talk about capitalism and how people don't care about the suffering they create if they can make a sweet profit off it. It is a common belief that animals serve human existence by providing us food and otherwise have no other purpose in "our" world. We lock them away in zoos for our entertainment and eat them for our pleasure. The treatment of animals and their habitats has caused numerous extinctions, as well as created many endangered species. The excuses for the treatment of animals can be related to the same excuses made to justify colonialism: "We are superior and know what this group needs better than they do." This excuse implies that humanity is some divine creature that was specifically made to control nature.

"On the Basis of Sex" (Patriarchy)
By *Caroline Borio*

The Hydra is a metaphor that represents the privileging forces that exist throughout the world, and more importantly, how they all interact. All heads share a common body, acknowledging that they all stem from the same source and they are all connected. One of the heads is the patriarchy, which Merriam Webster first defines as "social organization marked by the supremacy of the father in the clan or family, the legal dependence of wives and children, and the reckoning of descent and inheritance in the male line." However, I prefer their second definition, which defines patriarchy as "control by men of a disproportionately large share of power." ("Patriarchy.")

The patriarchy stems from sexism, which has led to the construction of gender roles and stereotypes about women and has prevented them from having the same rights as men throughout history. Women have had to fight for the right to vote, to work the same jobs as men, and so on. Even today, it's unconsciously presumed that a woman's job is to stay home and take care of the children while men go out and work. This is ever-present in our society, undeniably in the workplace, and there's a direct connection between this stereotype and the film *On the Basis of Sex*.

On the Basis of Sex explores the ideas of patriarchy and gender inequality as it follows the early life of Ruth Bader Ginsberg. However, before the film gets to the main plot, it shows how significant gender inequality was in Ginsberg's personal life. In one of the very first scenes, Ginsberg walks into Harvard Law School surrounded by only men, all carrying briefcases and wearing matching suits.

At the first dinner with the Dean of Harvard Law, he asks the women why they're at Harvard and "occupying a place that could have gone to a man." Finally, even after attending Harvard and Columbia, and graduating top of her class, Ginsberg is unable to get a job at a law firm, and instead takes a job as a law professor. Later in life, Justice Ginsberg said this about the experience: "I was Jewish, a woman, and a mother. The first raised one eyebrow; the second, two; the third made me indubitably inadmissible." (Thulin)

Even this early on, the movie demonstrates how sexist stereotypes and gender roles are present in our society and institutions. These assumptions can become incredibly harmful as they form a system of oppression that says women are less than men. That said, Ginsberg is an example of a woman who challenged the patriarchy by pursuing a career that is not traditionally a woman's "job," and used her career to challenge laws that differentiated based on sex.

The movie focuses on Ginsberg's first case, where a man named Charles Moritz was denied a tax deduction on caregiving expenses for his ill mother, even though this deduction was given to other people in his position. The law said the deduction was to be given to "a woman, a widower or divorce, or a husband whose wife is incapacitated or institutionalized," and Moritz was a single man who had never been married. (US Court) Ginsberg argued that this was discrimination based on sex, because women in the same circumstances would be given the tax deduction. Ginsberg believed this perpetuated the idea that women should be responsible for arranging caregiving, even though there is no reason a woman should be providing care more than a man. On its own, this case was important, but it was also the first step towards a larger goal. At the time, there were 174 laws that differentiated based on sex, and winning this case was Ginsberg's first step to taking down all laws that assume gender inequality. In her final statement in court in the movie, Ginsberg says, "Our sons and daughters are barred by law from opportunities based on assumptions about their abilities. How will they ever disprove these assumptions if laws like Section 214 are allowed to stand?" This assumption about abilities based on sex is at the foundation of the patriarchy, and creates gender inequality in our institutions, laws, and everyday life.

While *on the Basis of Sex* focuses primarily on sexism, relating it to the Hydra, it's important to remember that this is just one of many privileging forces that is based on the "othering" of a particular group. People of various races, gender identities, abilities, and more face similar situations in which they are "othered." While it may be impossible to kill the Hydra entirely, films like *On the Basis of Sex* remind us that it is critical to engage in an attempt of taming the Hydra to create a more equal, just world for everyone.

128

Chapter 15
Teaching an Online Sociology Course in Bangladesh

Posted on: July 31, 2021

Introducing 'Critical Hydra Theory'

My teaching assistants and I are just over halfway through our experimental 10-week short course 'Introduction to Sociology.' Our class is comprised of 20 learners, 14 of them are from Myanmar, Rohingya refugees in Cox's Bazar, and the other six are Bangladeshi nationals. The class also has a mix of males and females, though not unpredictably so males dominate in terms of numbers.

Three learners studying our text.
Photo used with permission.

Our class meets synchronously via Google Meets or Zoom for approximately one and a half to two hours each week. There are the usual technical difficulties on both ends, but in the refugee camp especially, Wi-Fi connectivity is iffy in the best of times and during times like the hard rains, the connections are sometimes poor or lost altogether. Also, as if on cue, the call to prayers comes through someone's microphone at least once every class. Keeping all 20 students for the full amount of time is pretty much impossible, but we are doing our best. In addition to the chronic Wi-Fi issues, my refugee learners are currently on lockdown because of Covid.

I have two extraordinary teaching assistants who help me with this class. Here in North Carolina, I have Trevor Molin, my former student. He volunteered to help with this class as part of the service component in my Global Social Problems class.

My other teaching assistant is Azizul Hoque, who has taken time off his other duties at the Brac University <u>Center for Peace and Justice</u> based in Dhaka to fix, translate, and otherwise make the class happen in Bangladesh. Without Aziz, the class could not happen. His ability to translate my sometimes-high-level vocabulary into the local language- both Bangla and Rohingya is nothing less than amazing; he never hesitates and rarely asks me for clarification. The three of us have a great working relationship and typically meet via WhatsApp several times each week both before and after our weekly synchronous class.

Members of our class in Cox's Bazar, Bangladesh
at orientation. Photo courtesy Azizul Hoque

Our text is an OpenStax free text -Sociology 2e- which I edited down from 450+ pages to about 140. We had this modified text printed and bound in Cox's Bazar and distributed to our students. I have asked them to read approximately one chapter per week and watch the four to five short videos that I create to add and clarify the content.

We have our challenges. But the overall vibe of the class is that our time together is extraordinarily valuable, and we all make an effort to do what we can to make our class happen. Bangladesh is many hours ahead of the US, so although we meet in the late afternoon for the learners, it is an early morning class for me and my teaching assistant Trevor. We get up at 5:00 or 5:30 am, start the coffee, and join the class at 6:00 am.

We had a good response to our mid-session student perception of teaching survey (80 percent) and overall earned very high marks. When asked: Overall how would you rate the experience in the course? 81 percent indicated 'very valuable', and the remaining 19 percent said, 'very valuable."

Another key question was: "Is this class relevant and useful to you?". Below is a screen grab of the results.

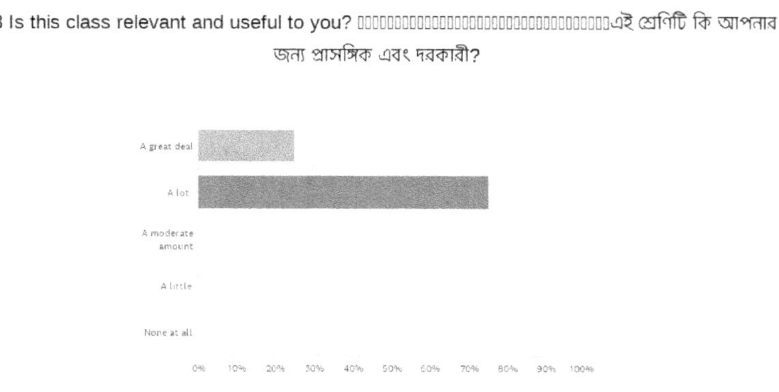

Used by permission.

Some background and context

I have been writing about and working with Rohingya refugees _for nearly two years now and my relationships led me to Jessica Olney, a fellow with the Center for Peace and Justice (CPJ) at Brac University in Bangladesh. Jessica visited my Global Social Problems class this spring at Elon University via Skype, and we talked about, among other things, creating an online class for refugees. Our plans became reality just after the end of Ramadan this spring when we started a grand experiment that is made possible only by support from Brac University the CPJ.

Currently across the globe, 80 million people have been forcibly displaced from their homes - about one percent of humanity - and at any time, approximately seven million people are living in managed refugee camps. The harsh reality is that the average stay in refugee camps is counted in years and even decades, not months or days.

The humanitarian organizations administering the refugee camps have all manner of tasks to accomplish to keep a camp functioning. Top on their priority list is safety and security, but <u>WASH</u>, shelter, food, and camp organization and communication are all very high priorities. Lower on the priority scale is keeping everyone occupied. In the case of adults, there are many '<u>cash for work</u>' programs where refugees work with NGOs to do necessary tasks around the camp. I have written about these refugees and have called them refugee humanitarians.

Younger people of course need to be taken care of, and there are various NGOs that focus on daycare, kindergarten, and primary education (e.g., Save the Children and World Vision). Secondary and tertiary education are far down on the priority list. That's where this class comes in. I am teaching both refugees and Bangladeshi nationals that are in their late teens and early 20s, hungry to learn, but with limited pathways to further themselves educationally. To my knowledge, ours is a unique class, bringing together refugees and nationals.

Toxic Othering

In class we talked about the content of Chapter 6 in their text (Social Organizations), and I was describing the basic sociological terms of 'in group' and 'out group.' I have not talked to them yet about the Hydra Model, but in a previous video lecture, I introduced the concept of 'othering.' In one of the classes, we talked about how one group tends to 'other' another group. I then went on to differentiate between 'normal othering' and 'toxic othering.' I described to them in simpler words, how much differentiation is different from stratification. That is, seeing differences is normal and typically okay, but using differences to justify seeing people as inferior or marginalizing them is bad, it is toxic othering.

'Othering'

The core process that generates
the privileging forces of the Hydra

A ≠ B

Group A is different from group B
Differentiation
'Normal/non-toxic othering'

A > B

Group A is superior to group B
Stratification
'Toxic othering'

After class, I talked to Aziz about how he explained othering in Bangla and the Rohingya language. He said that he had to first understand it himself, but through my examples where I talked about how one sports team is different from another sports team and seeing your team as naturally better is part of how we all function. We are all a bit ethnocentric, for the most part benignly so. In the same way, we can be a bit centered toward our other ascribed and achieved statuses, sometimes just 'normally' but all too frequently our othering become toxic, especially when there are scarce resources at play.

The same thing can be seen in the example of the family where families do things in slightly different ways. I made the point that it is a matter of perspective; we are the 'other' to those in different groups that we 'other.' People naturally see that groups can be different. Seeing and acknowledging these differences in others is normal othering. Toxic othering is seeing the other as inferior and not just different.

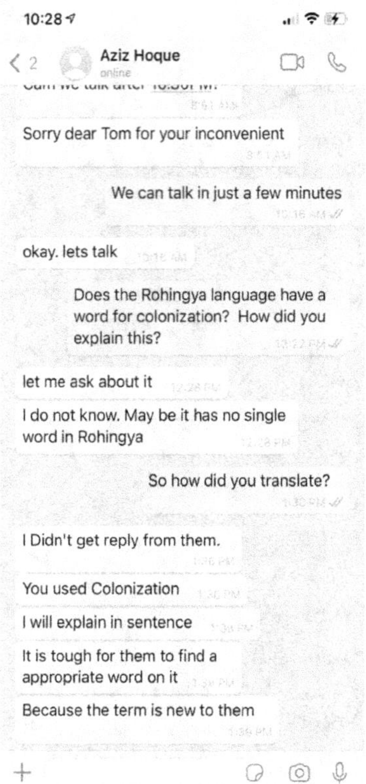

Screengrab of a WhatsApp conversation
with my translator Aziz.

Going to the macro level, I used the example of colonization as toxic othering on a global level, pointing out that the British colonization of much of India and Southeast Asia (and elsewhere, of course) was a classic form of toxic othering, where one group saw that they (British) were different from another and made the assumption that this made them superior to the other (those living on the subcontinent of India) and used that assumption to justify and rationalize the colonization of these people. The irony that I was conducting this class in English was offered as another example of an oppressive colonial legacy.

My teaching assistant and translator later told me that the Rohingya language has no word for colonization. I find this to be both disturbing and a bit surreal given the fact that their lives are impacted in such a major way by the legacies of colonial control.

Here is what my US teaching assistant Trevor Molin had to say about this class,

Yesterday, I learned that many of the individuals I've been helping teach don't have a word for colonizer in their language. A word that bears a history of hundreds of years of death and cultural erasure, a word so linked to the present conditions of these people, Bangladeshi and Rohingya alike. A word thrown around carelessly at times in the States, of a false identification of our forefathers as fighting against the colonial forces of the British Empire, when, all they truly did win was the autonomy of their colonial force. There are dozens of sayings speaking of the lessons that must be learned from the past, but for those learning in the virtual class with me today, a word doesn't even exist to identify one of the greatest drivers of the way that they live today.

This class has been eye-opening to me, particularly in learning about the cultural differences between myself and those who are being taught. Each day I learn another way in which our education differs, or norms differ, our families differ, and today, how our language differs.

At the end of the day, Aziz was able to convey the concept of toxic othering very well to all the learners, and I even had a couple of them give examples. One young woman talked about how the males in her life tend to see her as different and not as capable. Her father encourages her and sees her for the full human that she is, but he is an exception. A young man gave the example that as a Rohingya he was othered (also known as <u>genocide</u>) by people in Myanmar, in particular by the <u>Tatmadaw</u>, and that has led him to have to flee his homeland.

Here is how Aziz describes the challenge of translation,

"Being involved in the course, I realized that the success of learning depends on the use of appropriate language (e.g., first language) or medium of communication between learners and instructors and which helps learners to relate content to their context.

While I interpret, identifying appropriate words in the Rohingya language to translate, many English terms like culture, colonialism, and socialization were a regular challenge. Indeed, Rohingya is a dialectical language that does not have an available written alphabet. Therefore, it absorbed numerous foreign words e.g., Arabic, Urdu, Hindi, Bengali and Burmese and it has been a hybrid. Sometimes, I had to use one more word or small sentence and example to interpret a single English term. Before attending the session, I had to collect words on the subject either from Google or sometimes by asking my family and friends in Cox's Bazar to know how they use the words in their conversation. However, translating into Bengali was easier for me as it has the available vocabulary to interpret from any language."

I knew that this class would pose pedagogical challenges for me, and indeed it does, but my task is by far much easier than that of Aziz, he must not only understand the points being made but immediately find a way to translate these complex concepts into now one but two other languages. He handles this task with grace and unmatched professionalism in each class.

Critical Race Theory and Critical Hydra Theory

So yes, I was teaching Critical Race Theory in my sociology class. The Hydra Model is indeed a call to understand how privileging forces of patriarchy, race/ethnicity, hetero/cisnormativity, classism, ableism, ageism, and anthropocentrism have all been generated by toxic othering and are indeed impacting the lives of everyone on the planet, negatively so people like the Rohingya and other refugees around the world.

Critical Race Theory deals directly with one head of the Hydra but also, done well, emphasizes the inevitable and inherent intersectionality of racial and ethnic histories. You cannot effectively cover Critical Race Theory without talking about the history of toxic colonialism, for example. Critical Hydra Theory involves looking at how toxic and marginalizing othering is represented by all the heads of the Hydra and is evidenced in long-standing norms, policies, and laws that have normalized and justified various forms of discrimination, exclusion, marginalization, and even genocide, toxic othering. These socially structured inequalities exist in all cultures to varying degrees and so critical Hydra Theory is necessarily global and demonstratively historical in scope.

The overall intent of this certificate course is not to create 'mini sociologists', but rather better community leaders, with a deeper sense of who they are and the social forces that impact them and their communities. My deepest hope is that what we are learning in this class about various pedagogies, what works and what does not work, will eventually inform, and contribute to other classes being offered by faculty persons from around the world. I firmly believe that critical race theory - and critical Hydra Theory - have a central place in this and any future classes.

Chapter 16
Deepening our Understanding of 'Toxic Othering'

Blog post posted on: July 17, 2021

Teaching an introduction to sociology class to Rohingya and Bangladeshi learners is an amazing experience. This class has tested my abilities as an educator, and for that I am thankful. Explaining topics like ethnocentrism and othering most definitely have stretched the limits of my pedagogical skills.

In a recent post on my blog, I described how our class has gone thus far and ended with a discussion of 'Critical Hydra Theory'. I argued:

> *"Critical Hydra Theory involves looking at how toxic and marginalizing othering is represented by all the heads of the Hydra and is evidenced in long-standing norms, policies, and laws which have normalized and justified various forms of discrimination, exclusion, marginalization, and even genocide; toxic othering."*

In our WhatsApp chat, one of my students asked:

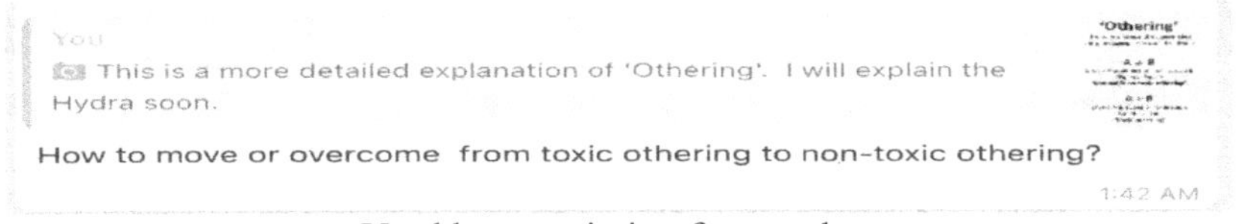

Used by permission from a chat.

"How to move or overcome from toxic othering to non-toxic othering?"

Student questions have always driven my analytical thoughts, and this one was truly inspirational.

Here is how I responded:

Picture used by permission.

Tin Swe is the learner who asked the great question. Here he is studying and taking notes from our text and a video. Photo submitted and used with permission.

"One of your classmates recently asked a wonderful and very important question on our WhatsApp group and I want to take a few minutes to talk about this question. The question had to do with othering and toxic othering. The question essentially was, "How do we change from toxic othering to non-toxic othering?" There couldn't be a better question, there couldn't be a more important question to focus on as we address the issue of our local problems and our international problems. The question is essentially about social change and how we can reconstruct some parts of our society which are toxic othering and address those norms and policies and laws and change them in a positive direction. An American cleric used the phrase' bending the moral arc of the universe' and he made the point that the direction of the moral arc is towards justice, and our job - these are my words - our job is to work in such a way that we move the directions of the moral arc towards justice. The moral arc of the universe is long, but it does - and I believe in this - bend toward justice. And what this means, what this justice means is a world where toxic othering has been eradicated [that] toxic othering of other genders, of other races, of other ethnicities, to other people in general, that toxic othering is eradicated from the earth. As such our job as social thinkers, our job as people

who are leaders in our community is to work in such a way such that we minimize toxic othering and maximize pathways that are non-othering [or rather] nontoxic othering. In short, getting rid of toxic othering is a huge job that we all need to participate in both on the individual level and on the organizational level. We need to encourage ourselves and everyone around us and all the organizations to which we belong. ... we need to have them move toward a nontoxic othering kind of set of norms, policies, and laws. Let us begin this journey together. (Here is the video version of my response.)

The original "moral arc" quotation comes from Theodore Parker, a Unitarian pastor in Lexington, Massachusetts. In an 1853 sermon, he preached *"I do not pretend to understand the moral universe; the arc is a long one, my eye reaches but little ways; I cannot calculate the curve and complete the figure by the experience of sight; I can divine it by conscience. And from what I see I am sure it bends toward justice."* The Reverend Dr. Martin Luther King, Jr. summarized that phrase into a shorter statement. He said, *"The arc of the moral universe is long, but it tends toward justice."* Former President Barack Obama also used the phrase in various comments and speeches.

We must understand power to tame the Hydra

One question raised by both quotations is whether or not the moral universe bends towards justice on its own or rather through collective human action. Typically, people that use the phrase indicate that we all need to work together to bend the moral arc toward justice; it is humans that will bending the arc.

In my case I have argued on both sides of the perspective. Sometimes I feel as if the human impact is superfluous and that it's an anthropocentric illusion that we control our world. Other times, when I am more optimistic, I believe that the moral universe is impacted by our actions to change norms, policies, and laws that allow for us to make many incremental changes that, taken together, make our world collectively more just.

Our amazing teaching assistant, Aziz Hoque from the Brac University Center for Peace and Justice, commented that the concept of power is essential in understanding othering. Though this idea has been implicit in how I have discussed othering and the Hydra thus far, I now know that going forward, explaining both images must make this more explicit. Included here are the updated versions.

In WhatsApp discussions about this topic, this is part of what I said,

> *"Even when there is a slight difference in power between two groups (A and B) normal Othering can turn into toxic Othering very quickly, and those in power enjoy their privilege so much that they find ways to make the power disparity permanent. Through this lens, we can look back at the entirety of human history and see how privileging forces have been woven into all aspects of every culture.*

'Othering'

The core process that generates the privileging forces of the Hydra

A ≠ B

Group A is different from group B
Differentiation
'Normal/non-toxic othering'

Whenever there is an asymmetry of power between A and B there exists a strong possibility that differentiation will morph into stratification.

A > B

Group A is superior to group B
Stratification
'Toxic othering'

And this book, Understanding and Taming the Hydra, *begins with the very simple premise that #MeToo, #BlackLivesMatter, #Decolonize, #ClimateCrisis, and so on are all rooted in the process of toxic othering which has been systemically embedded (to varying degrees) into all world cultures."*

Taming the Hydra means understanding and then deconstructing the toxic othering that has been done all through history. The counter forces that want to bend the moral arc in a negative, 'unjust' direction are strong, and they are represented in some of the leadership we have around the world right now. Look at what's happening in Ethiopia. Look at what is happening in Myanmar. Look at what is happening in Palestine. Look at what is happening in the United States. There are many forces, I have called them 'privileging forces,' that have been so woven into our cultures and nations around the world. Bending these, changing these, reforming these is tremendous work. Many fight this antitoxic othering work because they benefit, or they are driven by some base impulses, for example gluttony and greed.

Bending the moral arc toward justice, taming the Hydra, means an infinite number of small acts on each of our parts, all geared toward changing social norms and policies in the organizations with which we work in our communities, and laws at all levels local, national, and international. We need to raise our voices not just as informal agents of social control and social change but urge those who are formal agents of social change, our politicians and thought leaders in organizations and businesses. We need to urge all these individuals through phone calls, texts, emails, and one on one conversations to change policies and laws which contribute to toxic othering.

This path is difficult and fraught with cultural complexities. Some of our cultural norms and even our laws have demonized and marginalized some statuses. I know that it is going to be difficult for many to accept that, for example myopic heteronormativity, is a problem, and that acceptance of different sexualities and gender identifications is something that flies in the face of much cultural learning for many people around the world, especially so in cultures where religion is a core element.

Perhaps the biggest issue regarding toxic othering is related to anthropocentrism. We tend to see ourselves as of course dominant over nature, that is we 'other' nature, and this relationship is clearly one that is toxic both metaphorically and literally. Being anti-anthropocentric will be seen as anti-capitalism to many because it means re-thinking our concepts of comfort, progress, and 'lifestyle.'

I understand that this hill is a very steep one for many people, that being critical of one's own culture and traditions may seem unpatriotic or even heretical. Social change involving core institutions is contentious and well-meaning activists must be clear-headed, sober, and willing to be allies of and accept ally support from other diverse social justice movements, always with an eye toward the basic process of othering.

Bending the moral arc means confronting entrenched power wielded by all those who enjoy majority status privileges (male, white, Global North, cis/hetero/affluent, able, and non-old). Power is rarely yielded willingly;

there will be -as both history and the turmoil-filled present will testify-resistance.

Teaching Critical Theory,
a Reflexive Statement

As a decades-long member and past President of the Association for Humanist Sociology, I have been teaching Critical Theory my entire career in each of my sociology classes. With that said, I will emphasize that my journey understanding, critiquing, and addressing historical forces creating and supporting social injustices is ongoing.

Like most older, white, male, hetero, cis, able, and Global North persons, my personal experience with injustice is limited. My class background (my family was well below the poverty line for my entire youth) does give me experiential knowledge of this privileging force. Regarding this and all other privileging forces, I listen intently to and take the lead from those who have first-hand experiences regarding the marginalizing power of socially structured inequalities, reading and rereading histories focusing on and written by those most affected. By using a continually more finely informed understanding of the vast array of social injustices across the globe and back through time I hope to make a modest contribution to shining a light on and actively challenging all privileging forces.

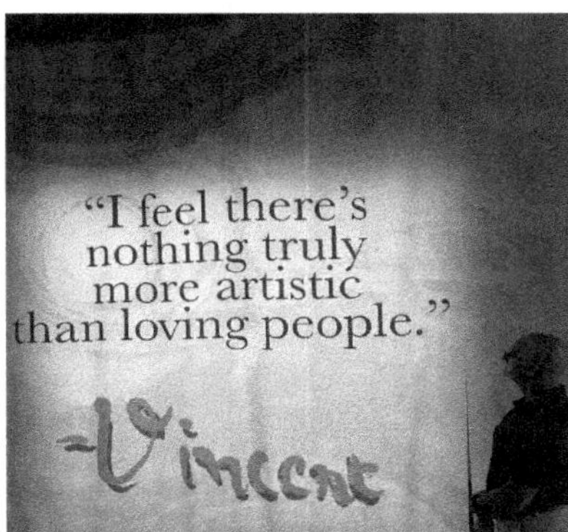

All that said, I am keenly aware that the trope 'Critical Race Theory' has taken on additional meaning in the last six months here in the United States as the political right condemns its teaching in high schools across our nation. By introducing the term 'Critical Hydra Theory' have I culturally appropriated this trope? I'll leave that question to the reader, but I will argue that most who are advocating for the teaching of Critical Race Theory would agree that separating racism from the other 'isms' is an intellectually and tactically weak perspective. To quote Cornel West, *'Justice is what love looks like in public.'* And justice never means 'just us' it means all who have been marginalized by any of the othering privileging forces.

And so perhaps West tells me I need to conclude by invoking an aphorism that has been oft repeated throughout history by the wise in all global cultures, religions, and thought systems: love is essential, love is the cure, love is the answer. It is the human capacity to love that will, finally, find a way to bring humanity together and tame the Hydra.

Final thank you to my learners in Bangladesh and Elon

Thank you to all the learners I have encountered online in Bangladesh and here at my university. I feel your passion and sense your compassion; you are the loving people who will join with others to create a more just world for all.

Chapter 17
Advanced Hydra Theory:
Understanding power and social forces

Blog post posted on: July 31, 2021

I am covering the chapter on social stratification with my Rohingya and Bangladeshi learners and I want to thank them as a group and especially our translator/teaching assistant Azizul Hoque from the Centre for Peace and Justice, Brac University for continuously inspiring my teaching and for providing excellent questions.

This discussion of stratification cuts to the heart of Hydra theory and its emphasis on privileging forces, and by probing deeply we can advance our understanding.

For decades in my intro to sociology classes I have summarized my longer and more technical definition of social stratification into just three words: structured social inequality. As I grappled with how to explain the phenomena of social stratification, I was forced to get to the fundamental nature of social inequality, that is, to get at the root of the issue, to get radical. Reflecting on our class' earlier conversations about othering and toxic othering, we were all forced to probe into a sober reality. Whenever there is an asymmetry of power in any social situation social differentiation can (must?) transition into stratification. This forces us to probe even deeper and thus deal with the concept of power. I explained to them that social powers are at play constantly and a good sociologist studies these social forces at both the micro (interpersonal) and the macro (community, organizations, and states) levels.

Refugee learner Shamima watching instructional videos
while writing notes and reading from our textbook.
Photo submitted and used with permission.

Here are the questions I posed in a short video message to my class ... and to myself as I continue exploring the concept of critical Hydra theory.

"As we discuss social stratification it is necessary for us to grapple with the concept of power. Power has been studied through time by all major sociologists, most particularly Max Weber who defined power as the ability to impose one's will over other people. And so, as we think about power, I want you to consider power in your life.

Who has power to make decisions that affect you: in your family, in your 'village', in your section of the camp, in the camp overall, in Bangladesh, in the Southeast Asian region, and globally? And considering each of these levels: Where did their power come from? How do those in control demonstrate their power (enforce their will)? What are the consequences when you or another person challenges their power? In your opinion do those in power at all these levels - the family, village, in the [refugee] camp, in Bangladesh, in Southeast Asia, and globally - do those in power act fairly? What are the consequences for you or others for 'speaking truth to power' that is confronting people when they are using their power incorrectly or in an unjust way? Another question to ask is how is their power used to support a concept we talked about in depth, 'toxic othering'?

What personal power do you have and how do you use it in your life? How do you use your power(s) to make your life better? How do you use your power(s) to make your family's life better? How do you use your power(s) to make your community's life better? How do you use your power(s) to make your village better? How do you use your power(s) to make Bangladesh or Myanmar better? How do you use your power(s) to make the world better?

Those are all very important questions that I just asked, and I don't expect everyone to answer them all, but I do want you to think about those questions, think about power swirling around you as you walk through the village, as you walk through the camp. Who has the power to control, who has the power to say what happens and what does not happen, and how did they get that power."?

In response to the video concerning power, my teaching associate Azizul Hoque received a reflection from a Bangladeshi learner while he was mentoring the cohort. The learner noted,

"People with money and political affiliation are considered as power holders regardless of their personality, education or capacity to guide the community properly. Poor villagers unquestionably accept the words and work of a local influential person as a guarantee as they can offer money to solve a social problem".

Azizul replied to the learner and observed,

"In an underprivileged area like Cox's Bazar, most people are politically unaware of where power lies, especially at higher levels. The inequality conversely paves the way for certain tiny classes such as rich peasants, the family whose sons or relatives are government officials, the local political cadre who receive government's contracts for

> *infrastructural development or relief distribution, these people are small in number and common people cannot deny their influence. It motivates the young of these families, who are outside the power block, to work for a wage or migrate to Middle Eastern countries as laborers. It emancipates some of them from poverty however the majority can hardly come out of this powerless cycle. Certain cultural bottlenecks exist such as malpractice of bureaucratic power, nepotism in resource distribution and petty corruption. Therefore, power is unequally distributed in the communities where money and muscles act as determinants and whereas the socio-economically impoverished/marginalized species of the community seem to be guaranteed.*
>
> *The power dynamics of a refugee community are very different from host communities."*

The list of power influences that Azizul notes is indeed a massive problem. Massive understatement: The corrupt actions of those who gain power leads to much social injustice and systemic marginalization, and understanding the full nature of the power dynamics of one's social position is frequently difficult if not at times impossible. This is in part because legitimate and illegitimate power sources can exist separately but also within the same organizational entity, for example a corrupt official within a legitimate organization.

One of my refugee learners asked,

> *"When an authority people say criminal to an innocent public as accusation, it is ok. When a civilian says ill about authority, it is a crime."*

He went on to give many other examples, each with the same theme, finally asking *"What's sociological views on this?"* Here is the gist of my response.

> *"These are all excellent questions and each one points to the question of power and how it is used. One social philosopher put it this way, "The ruling ideas of any age*

are ever the ideas of the ruling class." That is to say, those in power get to make the rules, and they sometimes (maybe frequently) make rules that justify their own power and also justify rules, norms, policies and laws that serve to marginalize other groups (that is, they use their power to engage in toxic othering).

'Othering'

The core process that generates the privileging forces of the Hydra

A ≠ B

Group A is different from group B
Differentiation
'Normal/non-toxic othering'

Whenever there is an asymmetry of power between A and B there exists a strong possibility that differentiation will morph into stratification.

A > B

Group A is superior to group B
Stratification
'Toxic othering'

The role of the sociologist is to objectively, systematically, and thoroughly describe, document, and analyze power: how it is gained, maintained, used, and abused. Using this information, the sociologist supports those who would challenge those in power when they are using their powers in harmful ways. Indeed, the reason d'être of sociology is to 'investigate humanity for the purpose of service.'

There are several aphorisms (sayings) that come to mind when talking about power. Perhaps the most often quoted is that "Absolute power corrupts absolutely." This 1887 statement by the British historian and moralist Lord Acton argues that as individuals gain power their sense of morality diminishes.

And this is how toxic othering leads to the marginalization of some lesser privileged groups: those in power, increasingly intoxicated by this power use their advantage to play on the insecurities of those 'beneath' them, making them feel inferior, thus setting in place a structure of power relationships that, over time, ossifies into permanence, becoming 'baked into' the culture. This process is at the origin of and indeed what fuels the body of the Hydra.

Yet another Brit, novelist and social critic George Orwell makes much of the concept of power in two of his most influential works, 1984 and Animal Farm. In the later book, the idea that 'power corrupts' is indeed the main message is illustrated in the book by a pig named, not coincidentally, Napoleon. The pigs, now in control of the farm and needing to explain why they have more power than the other animals, state that 'All animals are equal, but some animals are more equal than others.' *With this wording magic the transition from merely different (A≠ B) to being superior (A > B) is now complete.*

Another frequently mentioned quotation (though it may now have aged out of common usage) is "Power is the ultimate aphrodisiac." This statement is thought to be first uttered by the Frenchman Napoleon Bonaparte, but it gained much currency in the US in the late 1900's by American diplomat Henry Kissinger. Though the truth of this statement is suspect, the fact that men believe it to be true may help explain why some men seek power."

This last aphorism leads me to put weight on the conjecture that out of all the privileging forces, that of patriarchy (sexism) was the first to emerge and take root. In our species males wield physical power over women, and this asymmetry of power eventually was exploited in culture after culture. There is much written about the origin of patriarchy, some of it controversial, but that it exists now and is inextricably woven into the fabric of most existing cultures is a fact we cannot avoid. One premise of my thinking is that allowing for and justifying one form of structured social inequality provides normative support for the marginalization of some humans by others in their culture thus making it easier and perhaps inevitable that additional social status power differences be normalized. Restated, can it be argued, for example, that gender differentiation will lead to gender stratification and normalization of this social relationship gives license to additional toxic othering based on various status differences? I think yes.

Two refugee learners studying together.

Some basic sociology

One of our classmates asked this question,

> *Although social stratification is assumed as a system of inequality, why does everything [in] society support this system?*

My explanation to him was that yes, social stratification based on differences in status exists in virtually every culture, both past and present. But why? What is the social function of inequality? If social stratification is a cultural universal (true at least in the last several thousand years) why is this so? Other cultural universals like the family, religion, or art can be explained by how they function to maintain a culture's integrity, and perhaps this is so for structured social inequality.

The functionalist's logic goes like this. Using the organic analogy, there are no superfluous organs in the body; all the parts of the body's system are interdependent with all the other parts; every part of the body is there for a reason, and all the systems have a mutual goal, that is to keep the body functioning in a healthy fashion. The same is so in cultures. Cultures are integrated wholes where all the parts (i.e., social institutions like the family) are mutually interdependent and all geared to keep the culture running optimally.

So, is structured social inequality - a cultural universal- healthy for society?

The answer to this question is not simple, but the critical theoretical tension here is between the two main macro theories in sociology, namely functionalism and conflict theory. In question is whether or not social inequality, the unequal distribution of status and power, *is or is not* necessary and inevitable for cultures to function. The debate in sociology is more narrowly around the question of class, caste, and the distribution of economic power, but I argue that the underlying logic works for other privileging forces as well.

An American sociologist, Kingsley Davis, summed up the functionalist perspective in one sentence:

> *"Social inequality is thus an unconsciously evolved device*
> *by which societies ensure that the most important positions*
> *are conscientiously filled by the most qualified persons."*

Structured social inequality is necessary and inevitable, according to the functionalism perspective. In any culture there is a complex division of labor needed to get all necessary tasks accomplished and keep the culture running. Some jobs are more important than others and these jobs must be rewarded more highly in order to attract the most qualified individuals to do the job. Some people must be able to acquire more power and privilege than others to encourage them to take on the more critical tasks. Social inequality must be part of the structure of an optimally functioning culture, so says the functionalist.

The conflict perspective, implicitly adopted throughout my posts on the Hydra and in my discussions of toxic othering, is that social inequality is neither necessary nor inevitable to for a culture to function, and that a world without extreme social stratification can be made possible by human efforts to put in place norms, policies, and laws which embrace differentiation but reject toxic stratification. It is possible for humans to live in an essentially egalitarian world where there may be some meaningful yet moderate disparities of material wealth, but all members of the culture have access to basic needs and pathways to dignity.

Host learner Omme Habiba writing notes for class.

Ultimately Critical Hydra theory is an effort to reach what I define as the goal of humanitarianism: an ideology of human growth and potential based on the assumption that we should all be working toward a world where every human not only has pathways to but is actively encouraged to reach all their potentials, physical, mental, emotional, and spiritual. And further that these pathways acknowledge and respect the rights and needs of not only future human generations but other life forms as well.

The sociological debate historically has centered around social class differences, but the Hydra theory proposes synchronous and inherently intersectional othering processes related to gender, ethnicity, etc. and this toxic othering (the transition from differentiation to stratification) slowly and insidiously being normalized for all the heads of the Hydra. This quote from the original source of most conflict theory, Karl Marx, offers this summary explanation,

> *"The ruling ideas of each age have ever been the ideas of its ruling class."*

Social forces

In a video for the class I presented an equation explaining social stratification. In the very simplest form of this equation, I present one way to answer the question 'why are there rich and poor?'

Why are there rich and poor?

Simple explanation:

Poverty/Affluence = f (P * S) where

P = personal traits like a good work ethic, being frugal, being 'smart'
S = social structural factors like gender, race, or ethnicity

Critical Hydra theory explanation:

Poverty/Affluence = f (IC * PS * C [S +H + G]) * x where

IC = **Individual character** (e.g., work ethic, being frugal, being 'smart')
PS = Privilege score (based on the Hydra model and calibrated by location)
C = Chance (S = social, G = geography, and G = health)

X = other variables

Both equations as written infer that all variables have equal weight, which of course they do not. Weighting should be added as appropriate.

Poverty/Affluence = f (P * S) where

P = personal traits like a good work ethic, being frugal, being 'smart'
S = social structural factors like gender, race, or ethnicity

Put into words, Poverty or Affluence of a person is a function of two general variables namely personal qualities (or lack thereof) and social structural factors.

The Critical Hydra Theory explanation is more detailed.
Poverty/Affluence = f (IC * PS * C [S +H + G]) * x where

IC = Individual character (e.g., work ethic, being frugal, being 'smart')
PS = Privilege score (based on the Hydra model and calibrated by location)

C = Chance (S = social, H = health, G = geography)
X = other variables

Put into words, Poverty or Affluence of a person is a function of individual character, the privilege score of the individual (where all the heads of the Hydra represent various statuses, and chance factors such as social context (e.g., number of siblings, birth order, social relationships, and so on), health (mental, emotional and physical), and geography (where a person is born/lives, e.g., urban, rural, and a myriad of other dimensions).

Both equations as written infer that all variables have equal weight, which of course they do not. And demonstratively so, weighting matters a great deal. Using the simpler model to explain poverty or affluence, the question to ask is that if these two variables (P and S) are not equal, which should be weighted more, which is the more influential variable?

Those who defend the stratification system, mostly the rich, will argue that P is more important and that they are in their position because of a strong work ethic and in general being frugal and smart, that is, superior humans. The poor tend not to blame themselves and thus see S as being the dominant variable by far though acknowledging the influence of personal effort.

The Critical Hydra Theory view is that not only one's relative wealth but more than that, what sociologist Max Weber called one's 'life chances', are determined mostly by social forces and hence the simple equation would look more like this:

$P/A = f(P * 10S)$, with poverty or affluence ten times more influential than personal character.

In sum, all humans are impacted by power and the social forces put in play by the use and abuse of power by individuals and groups who find a way to exploit differences and turn differentiation into stratification. Personal character matters, but it is far outweighed by many external variables, mostly privileging forces.

Power and social forces

The dynamic described above, allowing for the marginalization of some humans by others, has played out throughout human history. Structured social inequality is the product of toxic othering, itself the product of the perhaps inexorable process of status differences being used to justify the inferior treatment of those deemed 'less equal.'

Critical Hydra theory demands an understanding of power and the social forces that lead to structured social inequality. But looking at only the present is not enough, the critical Hydra theorist must look deep into the history of each culture, this task becoming increasingly difficult as the process of globalization accelerates.

Thank you

I'll conclude by again thanking the 20 learners - 14 Rohingya refugees and six host community Bangladeshis - in Bangladesh joining me in this journey of exploration and understanding. Their inspiring questions continue to push our analysis and understanding forward. Critical Hydra theory is maturing because of this special class of women and men, some refugees, other members of the host community, all joining together to move themselves and all of humanity in a more positive direction.

Chapter 18
Retroactive application of critical Hydra theory

Blog post originally posted August 2021

As I approached the task of talking explicitly and in detail about the Hydra with the learners in Bangladesh, I found myself going back to my 'greatest hits', ideas that had stead me well over the decades teaching sociology to mostly privileged US undergraduates.

Rohingya learner taking notes from Introduction
to Sociology text.

I realize now, more deeply than I'd like to admit, I was part of a culture that taught about power and privileging in a very traditional way, that is to say ignorant to the history of how deeply and thoroughly asymmetrical and toxically marginalizing power had been embedded itself into every fiber of all world cultures. I knew the world was not fair but had not demanded of myself an examination of my own blinders and preconceptions. Knowing something in the abstract is very different from experiencing it in real time discussing topics with my learners.

A quick point, though. We are all creatures of the culture in which we were born, the *weltanschauung* in which we were socialized, our way of understanding the world absorbed deeply into our consciousness. In his book Ishmael Daniel Quinn uses with great effect the image of 'Mother Culture' whispering into our ears, providing each of us many subtle but critical unwritten assumptions about our world. Our common task is to learn the ability to be critical of ourselves and the culture in which we live. Indeed this is the very reason I have taught this and all of my classes for the last 40 years about C. Wright

Mills' sociological imagination, about how to see the world beyond the lenses of our own culture. But this task is not easy or without risk. As anthropologist Jules Henry put it long ago, *"To look closely at our culture is to grow angry and to anger others."*

My colleague Azizul and I talked about how gaining critical thinking skills was indeed one of the main goals we had for our learners and how using these skills in daily life may set some of them apart from their peers, making them 'deviants'. Through history successful agents of social change have always been positive deviants, and we talked to the learners about how those fighting for democracy now in Myanmar are exactly that, women and men going against what the government says in order to fight the injustices and oppression. Given the in depth and frank discussion of gender-based violence (GBV) we had in our recent class session -many of the comments going from the females in class - I am confident this cohort of learners has the courage to, as appropriate, speak true to power. I have not urged them to cause 'good trouble' as John Lewis would say, but I am not doubting some may choose this path.

Learners or students?

Why use the word learner as opposed to student? When we were planning our first communications for our class, I referred to our 'students' but my colleague Azizul shared that the word 'learners' would be more appropriate. I had seen this term used in various international contexts but always defaulted to the US norm of using 'students'. I researched the difference and found that the learner, as defined in this graphic, perfectly described my hopes for those who are in my classes, learns anywhere (!), at their own pace, motivated by the desire to learn and so on. Though Azizul liked and shared this distinction between student and learner, his explanation as to why we need to use learner points out a political and diplomatic reality.

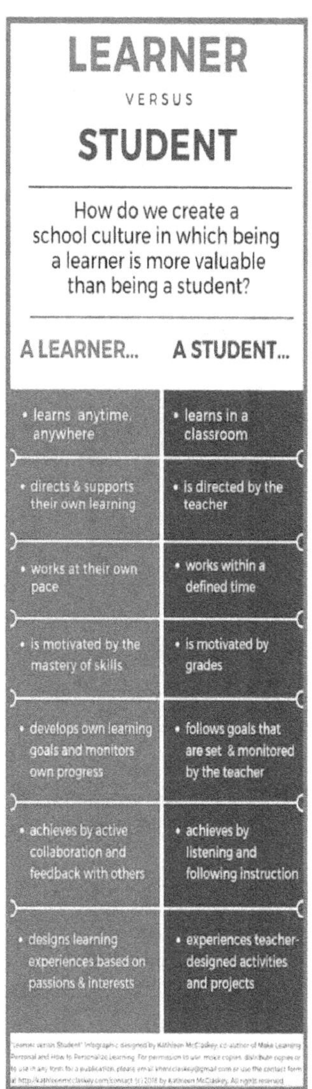

Image describing the difference between student and learner.

"We do not use student publicly for a couple of reasons. "Student" is related to a formal academic activity like school, working toward a degree in Bangladesh. On the other hand, Rohingya are not allowed to access formal education so far. However, they are allowed informal skill-

> *building workshops, training, and learning initiatives. Therefore, we called our Rohingya either volunteers or learners. On the other hand, learners implies a more self-driven approach whereas the student is top down. Thus, using learners, we wanted to make them proactive in learning. We do not teach however we facilitate their teaching-learning process. We learn collectively."*

There is much already written - with much more to come from both academic researchers and from those affected - about the many truncated rights of refugees, but our current experience with this cohort of learners highlights the limitations on the right to advanced education. This is an inherently political issue deserving of careful discussion at the highest levels.

Azizul, Trevor, and I have been interacting with a mixed group for the last several months - 14 Rohingya refugees and six Bangladeshi nationals, males and females in each sub-group. As a statement of fact, some in our class have more rights than others. That this is so in itself a delicate issue, one that I feel we have handled with utmost care, modeling a hyper conscientious egalitarian approach to all our class interactions.

Retroactive application of critical Hydra theory

As I write this, Taliban forces reacting to the power vacuum created by the US withdrawal are retaking much of Afghanistan by force. Primarily controlled by the men from one Pashtun ethnic group, the Taliban is a political movement that has altered world history by its use of violence against both outsiders and those within who would rebel.

But see what I just wrote? A 'traditional' statement about the Taliban which, looking now through the lens of critical Hydra theory, I argue glosses over the centuries (millennia?) old baked in misogyny which has subjugated women into second class persons. I will die on this hill: the treatment of women under the Taliban is not, as a cultural relativist might say, benign gender differentiation. We need to describe it as it is, stripped of male dominated cultural justification. Taliban treatment of women is overtly and toxically gender stratification.

Here is what I wrote nearly 40 years ago on this general topic. I have indeed come full circle.

> *"To thoroughly embrace the idea of relativism is to rationalize and justify a repressive and even destructive status quo in most cultures, at the very least with respect to the way women are treated."*

There is an old story from anthropology that I sometimes tell my students about how ethnocentrism is a cultural universal; all human groups have pride in themselves and tend to see 'others' as less than. Back to the basic definition of ethnocentrism as

"If A ≠ B therefore A > B."

The story comes from the British Anthropologist E. E. Evans-Pritchard described his study of the Nuer in East Africa, asking them what the word their people used for their culture "Naath" meant. Their response was that it meant "the people." Prichard asked for clarification, pointing out that though he was not Nuer but was not Nuer. They replied politely, 'no you are not people, you are not quite human.'

As I pointed out to my Bangladeshi learners, the line from othering to ethnocentrism is direct, as is the line from ethnocentrism to racism. Through the entirety of human history cultures like the Nuer have embedded a low-grade version of racism into their world view, this becoming more toxic as we see the long, bloody global history of slavery and genocide in not just the continent of Africa but in much of the rest of the world.

The line from othering to genocide,
from normal othering to toxic othering

- Othering can lead to ethnocentrism

- Ethnocentrism can lead to racism

- Racism can lead to dehumanization
  and counter anthropomorphization

- Dehumanization can lead to genocide

This is the image I shared with the learners in my video presentation on the line from othering to genocide.

Learning critical thinking skills and how to apply critical Hydra theory.

Human character is not a monolith, and there is a range of personality types which appear to exist among humans. Though necessary perhaps for group fitness in early epochs of our existence during the period of our development as a species, the existence of a personality type which enjoys power and control seems evident. Just as we find handedness to be a cultural universal - most efficiently explained using the concept of group (not individual) fitness - the same is so for the small but significant percentage of the population with a strong need for power.

As we transitioned from mostly egalitarian hunting and gathering lives (through several stages) to agricultural lifestyles, the problem of how to distribute the surpluses generated by the domestication of both plants and animals was solved by those who wanted power by creating and justifying various forms of social stratification. These personality types have long dominated the global landscape, and by looking at their movement through history we can see the bloody consequences of colonization driven by the lust for power these men had/have. Our poster child example here is perhaps King Leopold of Belgium who is responsible for the decade long genocide of perhaps 10,000,000 Congolese in the late 1800's. Leopold has much competition for his ignoble title of worst, as we turn to Mao, Pol Pot, Hitler, and others.

Back to the Taliban, their leadership, by systematically only pulling from one ethnic group, both outwardly and inwardly show overt signs of ethnocentrism, but a thinly veiled racism. The Taliban appears to be primarily controlled by the men from one Pashtun ethnic group. To be clear, the Taliban have hijacked Pashtun and Afghan culture, and cancerous misogynistic, racist, and classist privileging forces have taken root. The story of the racist and misogynistic Taliban is neither new nor uncommon; it can be seen countless times in cultures long before they came into existence and other examples fill every corner of the entire globe.

And so, we now see that the three main privileging forces representing the key 'isms' taught in most intro to sociology classes are all embedded inextricably in all world cultures. Race, gender, and class dynamics are central to most of the socially structured inequality we find virtually everywhere. These three privileging forces continue to work in tandem with each other and all the other privileging forces to sustain the many layers of marginalization which characterize human life. In the last several centuries the internal logic of capitalism and, more recently neoliberalism, have exponentially amplified all these forces, especially so classism.

An application of critical Hydra theory to our global history demands deconstructing our species' history of toxic othering and how these acts of marginalization have been normalized and even glorified by leaders, past and present. This deconstruction effort is not easy, fast, simple, nor uncontroversial, but taming the Hydra, I believe, can be accomplished.

Chapter 19
The root causes of toxic othering:
Narratives of Rohingya and Bangladeshis

Blog post originally posted August 18, 2021
Guest post by Mohammad Azizul Hoque

Ascribed status and identity politics

"Why have I become a stateless refugee in a world of 195 countries? Why have I been confined by persecution in my motherland Myanmar and beyond? I ask my friends and family, but none of them can soothe my inquisitive mind." A Rohingya refugee asked this question while Professor Thomas Arcaro and I were facilitating an online sociology course for underprivileged refugees and host community youth in Cox's Bazar, Bangladesh.

"Our hopes and aspirations are identical to other human species of the earth; however, because of our ethnicity, we are rejected, displaced and persecuted," commented another student.

Their words triggered us to apprehend how the ascribed status of "Rohingya" has become the cause of needless discrimination. Professor Arcaro replied, "Being a refugee or stateless is an ascribed status which you neither earned nor chose. Rather, it has been determined by the dominant groups in society and as a result, minorities are often assigned lower statuses." A Bangladeshi participant said, "Life under an ascribed status is not a bed of roses, but one of terrible spikes and fences." Toxic ethnocentrism-fueled identity politics based on language, religion, and ethnicity in Myanmar, which manifested in reaction to deliberate political and military maneuvers, have been largely backed by the Bamar (or Burmese) majority polity of Myanmar, a diverse nation comprised of hundreds of ethnic groups.

Iris Marion Young (1990) said that ascribed status of a minority ethnic group like the Rohingya makes them vulnerable to cultural imperialism (including stereotyping, erasure, or appropriation of one's group identity), violence, exploitation, marginalization, and powerlessness. Similarly, Francis Fukuyama (1992) addressed religion and nationalism as the two leading components of identity politics. Robert H. Taylor (2005) articulated that, after independence of 1948, Burmese's ruling forces were generous in handling the rights of the Arakanese Rohingya. However, in 1962, a new political transformation occurred when the Burmese military took over the political administration in a coup and embarked on a decades-long period of totalitarian rule, characterized by discriminatory campaigns against the country's non-Bamar groups.

Consequently, the military's ethnocentric identity politics led to the annulment of citizenship and nationality of Rohingya, and ultimately led to their deportation and ethnic cleansing.

Ethnocentrism, exclusion, and power distance

"Social power and resources are unequally distributed in our society," a Bangladeshi female student said. "Whether it's monsoon flooding, pandemic, or political instability, the destitute are always more affected than social elites, who can use their money and power to overcome crises. The peripheral people cannot overcome the effects." Here, social elites are privileged not only due to their wealth but also their membership in different dominant groups such as ruling parties, majority ethnic groups, affiliations with dynastic political and business families, roles in public administration, and other politico-economic associations. They often misuse their political power and commit nepotism to seize social resources; on the other hand, people at the bottom of the power hierarchy accept these imbalances as foregone.

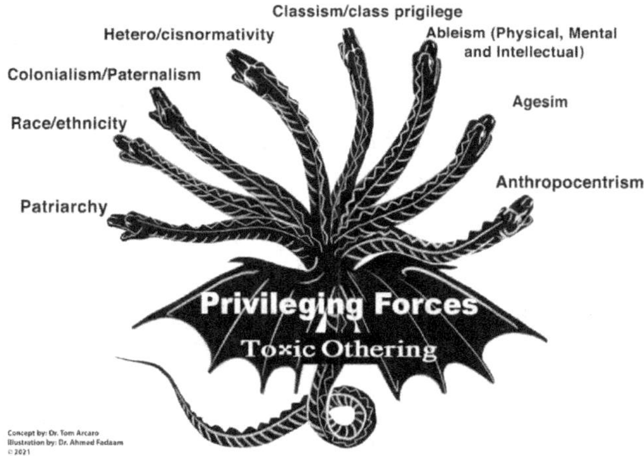

In a society where corruption is deep-rooted, a citizen hesitates to approach powerful bureaucrats and political representatives to claim the civic services to which they should be entitled. A Bangladeshi participant said, "If we challenge the roles of social elites, they may retaliate violently." In other contexts, disenfranchisement is legally enshrined altogether. In Myanmar, stateless Rohingya lack even basic legal entitlements to protection by the state, driving an intoxicated sense of impunity amongst the vigilantes and extremists who commit atrocities against them. Ethnocentrism has mushroomed alongside toxic othering so that Bamar Buddhists, the majority, are perceived and promulgated as the superior ethnicity. As a Rohingya student said, "Powerful groups use religion to justify the claim that other ethnic groups, such as Hindus, Muslims, Sikhs, Jains, and other religious minorities, are of foreign origins and have not been recognized as identity groups with rightful claims to Burmese nationality."

Through Facebook and national media outlets, the state has deliberately inflamed anti-Rohingya hate speech and propaganda towards the "othered," non-recognized groups, particularly followers of Islam (Reuters, 2018). A Rohingya student said, "In Rohingya areas, the military regime localized and tailored its human rights abuses and discriminatory rule by imposing restrictions on religious conversion and inter-faith marriage." Extremist nationalist propaganda functions to validate the fears harboured by the majority Buddhist population about the threat of a Muslim takeover of the country. As it transmits propaganda, the state implicitly sanctions social prejudice and inter-communal violence against Muslims (CFR, 2020). Another Rohingya student said, "Both communities (ethnic Rakhines and Muslims) feel that 'the other' is threatening to their identities, particularly their religion and culture." The key contestations have always been around equality (how power and resources are shared) and acceptance (how ethnic, religious, and cultural identities are respected (UNDP & Search for Common Ground, 2015).

Ideological divide and confrontational politics in Bangladesh

Confrontation, hatred, and blame games have been a common practice in Bangladeshi politics. Members of the "big others" (a small group in terms of the money and muscle power they hold) dominate the "small others" (who are large in size but remain at the bottom of the power hierarchy) through policy and law and by manipulating the state apparatus in their own favor. Political leaders have carried out elements of toxic othering at the local level in the name of both pro and anti-liberation movements, as well as religious ideologies, which are transmitted from the centre toward the periphery as tools to manipulate voters.

Broadly described, these othering processes feature a wide array of confrontation, competition, and monopolization of state institutions and resources by the party in power, which uses every possible state apparatus to marginalize the opposition (Arfina Osman, 2010). This trend has tremendously weakened formal accountability mechanisms, escalated a sense of impunity among political cadres, and put governance in crisis.

Bangladesh has earned remarkable GDP growth and infrastructure development in recent years; however, the gaps between wealthy and destitute have escalated simultaneously.

A Bangladeshi student said, "As power has been an effective tool of wealth accumulation, youths of middle and lower classes – particularly from urban areas – have become desperate to join government services or politics by any means." Political leaders personalize state power by creating networks and alliances to meet their objectives (Islam, 2013). Another Bangladeshi female student said, "If there are two candidates in a municipal election, people will vote for the high-income candidate despite his poor education, competency and honesty." Voters think that only the wealthier are capable of donating relief-good if they are affected by cyclone or flood. Hoque (2016) argued that some cunning candidates struggle to manipulate large poor voters with lump sums incentives like straight cash, token-money, wheat or rice as a shortcut tool of clientelism ahead of election. On the other hand, during the national election, mainstream political parties become desperate to win by hook or by crook. Because banally winner takes all and they monopolize state apparatuses with politically affiliated people.

Gender-based discrimination and false concepts of women's role in society

From a symbolic perspective, patriarchy has been a powerful privileging force in Rohingya and Bangladeshi families living in Cox's Bazar that results in gender-based discrimination, violence and marginalization. Unlike in more central areas, women in outlying and rural areas tend to be exceedingly underprivileged and suffer from poor health, illiteracy, and lack of participation in social and political decision-making, which persists in many spheres and poses particular challenges. "Rohingya women have forgotten how to speak publicly," a 20-year-old female refugee student said. "Our women and girls are always excluded from decision-making forums, either in the home or in the social sphere. Neither family nor community elders think it significant to take girls' consent on social and cultural matters." A recent study (Olney and Hoque, 2021) addressed the escalation of gender-based violence in Rohingya families during the pandemic. A Rohingya woman said, "We, as women, are always the victims of domestic violence when there is any misunderstanding or impoliteness between a wife, her husband and in-laws."

In many cases, false consciousness is the root cause among Rohingya refugees and Bangladeshi host families in Cox's Bazar where some people think that "Men have inherent authority to beat their women to correct their behavior," according to one student. "Gender inequality starts from men's toxic mind-sets." A refugee student said, "Women have to talk in a lower voice, always. Their husbands could get angry even if their wife expresses that she is ill."

Some students commented that societal discrimination against women leads families to marry off underage daughters as a strategy to ensure their protection, further compounding the same subjugation they hope to avoid. As another female student said, "Parents are prompted to marry off their daughter's right after puberty, because they are concerned for their security and economic burden." These dynamics consequently escalate the power distance between sexes, where women remain at the bottom of the power hierarchy and continue to be obstructed from accessing basic rights and education. "Men torture their wives whenever their parents disagree with her about something, or when he orders her to bring something to him from her parents and she can't bring it due to poverty." Bangladesh has formulated various laws, policies, and affirmative actions for women, which have significantly reduced the rate of violence against women, but there is still much room for progress.

Toxic othering as a colonial legacy

From a comparative perspective, Bangladesh and Myanmar are confronting different challenges; however, their underlying politico-cultural pathologies are identical. Both countries were colonized by the British Indian Empire, which cultivated toxic othering between communities through divide and rule policies, which systematically broke up larger concentrations of power into pieces that individually had less power than the implementer of the strategy, enabling the empire to secure its dominion (Christopher, 1988).

'Othering'
The core process that generates
the privileging forces of the Hydra

A ≠ B
Group A is different from group B
Differentiation
'Normal/non-toxic othering'

*Whenever there is an
asymmetry of power between
A and B there exists a strong possibility
that differentiation will morph
into stratification.*

A > B
Group A is superior to group B
Stratification
'Toxic othering'

The British purposely created fractions between ethnic, religious, and linguistic minorities in the occupied territory by promoting prejudice and toxic othering, destroying congenial relations between groups, gerrymandering geographic polities, and denying traditions to distract populations with infighting amongst themselves that prevented them from uniting in order to challenge the regime. Indian scholar and politician Shashi Tharoor (2017) write that the creation and perpetuation of Hindu-Muslim antagonism in British India was one of the most significant accomplishments of British imperial policy: the "divide et impera" (divide and rule) strategy facilitated continued imperial rule and reached its tragic culmination in 1947. Until 1857, there were no communal problems in India (Katju, 2013). Katju notes that although there were differences between Hindus and Muslims, with Hindus going to temples while Muslims went to mosques, participating in different festivals, and members of the two groups always helped each other and held no animosity.

Conclusion

A Bangladeshi participant said, "I wish I were able to defeat privileging forces." In response to that, Professor Arcaro said, "I have realized that The Hydra, or privileging forces, never end in Myanmar or in Bangladesh. It is a cultural universal. However, we can pacify the hydra to make it more innocuous." A refugee participant commented on the intergenerational transfer of the Hydra's power in Myanmar: "While General Ne win was brutally persecuting Rohingya people, our people thought that if he retired, the atrocities would stop. However, Ne Win has now gone, but many subsequent hostile persecutors have emerged." Now, efforts to mainstream social cohesion can contribute to a nation's resilience in the face of internal divisions and conflicts. Such efforts have the potential to present a more coherent vision of a nation's future to its diverse peoples.

Mohammad Azizul Hoque is a Research Associate at Centre for Peace and Justice, Brac University. He worked with Professor Thomas Arcaro as an interpreter for Bengali and Rohingya speakers and as a co-teacher of Sociology.
Email: azizul.hoque@bracu.ac.bd

Chapter 20
Talking with Rohingya and Bangladeshi learners about taming the Hydra

Blog post originally posted August 2021

> *"The educator has the duty of not being neutral."*
> -Paulo Freire

Taming the Hydra

My experience teaching sociology to Rohingya and Bangladeshi has been deeply rewarding. Introducing the ideas of culturally embedded privileging forces, ascribed statuses, toxic othering, and the image of the Hydra as a way to understand the common sources of various systemic affronts to human dignity has been an amazing and profound experience.

In our final class as we talked about taming the Hydra and false consciousness the learners offered many useful questions, comments, and examples. When we started this journey together several months ago, I had no expectation that given the language difficulties we would ever advance this far. That our last class was so engaging is a testament to my colleague Azizul's ability as a translator and critical thinker and even more so to the deep thirst for knowledge and insight shown by each class member.

> **Do we have a duty to use our sociological understanding of ourselves and of the world around us for the benefit of humanity? What is your understanding of the humanitarian imperative?**
>
> **All of these mean the same thing:**
> - Understanding and taming the Hydra =
> - Bending the moral arc toward justice =
> - Being a positive agent of social change working for the betterment of all humanity
>
> **Steps to take in order to work toward these goals:**
> - Constantly seek to learn more about yourself and the larger world around you. Learning never ends.
> - Be an ally to others if you are in a position of privilege and allow others to be an ally to you if you are being marginalized.
> - Seek ways to affect positive change in cultural norms, policies, rules, and laws at all levels -local, national, international.
> - "Be the change you want to see in the world"
> - Always choose love and compassion over hate and toxic othering.
> - When possible, make 'good trouble'; be a positive deviant.

The handout we used began with what by now the learners understood to be a rhetorical question, 'Do we have a duty to use our sociological understanding of ourselves and the world around us for the benefit of humanity?' Throughout our class and in my writing, I have used interchangeably the phrases 'taming the Hydra' and 'bending the moral arc toward justice', equating them both with the idea that as humanitarians we should be positive agents of social change.

I never explicitly covered the concept of intersectionality with reference to the eight heads of the Hydra in our class. Perhaps in an advanced class I can begin to probe the many possible combinations of marginalized statuses, and how one can -and often is- both in a position of being marginalized and in a status-superior position. That said, I got a clear sense from the male learners that they understood that though some were victims of paternalism/colonization while at the same time in a male dominated culture which systematically marginalizes females. Through this and other discussions both Azizul and I sensed that the learners intuitively understood the basic idea of intersectionality, that one's array of statuses are interrelated and have powerful additive and multiplicative connections deeply impacting their life chances. Here is what one Rohingya learner said,

> *"Hydra has many facets or aspects, especially difficult or intractable ones. I feel many deep complicated challenges ... and difficulties to tame hydra. Privileging forces are all interconnected. In some time, it can in turn create a great amount of toxic synergy. Likewise, there are some hydra-headed people who dominate many groups to support his acts and interconnected between them close. If we take action and destroy one head, the rest come up energetically to harm more because they are interconnected."*

Working to reverse false consciousness

We reviewed the argument that all of the heads of the Hydra are powered by the process of toxic othering and that led to introducing the concept of false consciousness. This idea was originated by Karl Marx and has been primarily used to describe classism in action. Other sociologists use the concept in various broader contexts and in very powerful ways. In my classes I have used the phrase 'socialization for disadvantage' to describe how false consciousness develops among various groups, most specifically females. False consciousness is the idea that those who are marginalized, those who are ascribed a lesser status by society, can come to believe that this lower status is just, proper, reasonable, and inevitable. They believe that they are inferior to the group that defines them as being inferior, i.e., they show a lack of an objective awareness of one's own potentials and abilities.

Jannatul Naem   7:25 AM
Women believe that they are not as smart or
as capable as men. The main reason for this
is that through affects a girl from an early
childhood through her family. When a girl
sees that men have been giving more priority
in every activity of the family she has come to
believe that girls are weak. For example – a
girl does not get the same support as boys
from the family for higher education. There
are many reasons why girls think they are not
equal to boys.
I think this is a false consciousness.

Here is what Jannatul wrote into the chat box in our last class

> *For example, women believe that they are inferior to men and believe that they are not as smart or as capable as men. Why would they believe that? If all the agents of socialization (family, peers, religion, media, education) either directly or indirectly are telling young girls that they are inferior they will tend to believe this culturally perpetuated untruth. False consciousness can be addressed and reversed by education, awareness, and by support from allies, support from, in this example, men treating women as equals.*

When a woman alone sees herself as inferior it's hard for her to act. But when she talks with other women and finds out that many feel the same, that women are being defined as inferior but really are not, when they begin to realize that they have some allies among men, their false consciousness can transition into class consciousness. When this begins to happen, when women in general believe that, yes, we are equal, then they begin to move for cultural changes that insure there are norms, laws, and policies that treat women on a more equal basis. Cross culturally we know that many forms of false consciousness exist relative to all the privileging forces, but they can be reversed and turned into class consciousness through awareness, education, and critical thinking.

Each of the heads of the Hydra, each of the privileging forces encourages various levels of 'false consciousness'. Marginalized class, gender, and race/ethnicity and religious statuses are more obvious, but clearly the same phenomena happen with all the other heads. Here are several examples.

- Paternalism, where the colonized feel inferior to those who 'gave' them their freedom, is being addressed broadly by many and very intensely in the humanitarian sector where 'decolonize aid' has become much more than a hashtag. This movement shows significant synergy with the global #BLM movement and stresses the intersectionality of race and class.
- Non-hetero/cis individuals in many (most?) cultures have historically been forced to hide their identities, their cultures socializing them to believe that they are not normal, defective, and morally sick. Forward movement on LGTBQI issues is uneven throughout the globe, with many in the majority world (Global South) suffering persecution and stigmatization.
- Differently abled persons - physically, cognitively, and emotionally- continue to be marginalized globally, but in this specific case there is both consciousness raising among those impacted by ableism and by the strong and increasingly vocal array of allies, many of them family members.
- Dire news about the climate crisis from respected experts has begun to address our species hubris, directly questioning the assumption that humans are superior to all other life forms and as such have the right to use and abuse the resources of the planet solely for our benefit.

Those that perpetuate false consciousness of any kind fuel the Hydra. Ethnocentrism can lead to racism and racism frequently, though perhaps not always, can lead to dehumanization and counter anthropomorphization. i.e., taking away the human qualities of some racial, religious, or ethnic group. When you dehumanize another group, when you take away their humanity it is as if you are just killing an animal or sub-human entity. Dehumanization can lead to the justification of genocide.

This is the image I shared with the learners in my video presentation on the line from othering to genocide.

The line from othering to genocide,
from normal othering to toxic othering

- Othering can lead to ethnocentrism

- Ethnocentrism can lead to racism

- Racism can lead to dehumanization
  and counter anthropomorphization

- Dehumanization can lead to genocide

The Hydra model demands that we also include all other marginalized statuses (e.g., gender) in this logic; toxic othering of any kind can lead to dehumanization and even to genocide.

I will continue to argue that using the Hydra is an effective way to understand the history of the world in terms of all the marginalizing and privileging forces which create inequalities between groups. All this toxic othering can spiral down into dehumanization and to genocide or at least into forms of subjugation and slavery. When you combine toxic othering with the concept of false consciousness this creates a situation where the people that are marginalized don't fight back because they believe that it is just that they are being marginalized. Taming the Hydra means understanding the need to educate people, facilitating the transition from false consciousness - believing that what is happening to them is right and just - to class consciousness where they reject dehumanization and marginalization. Often this means questioning many long held cultural norms and practices.

Bending the moral arc toward justice means understanding and recognizing how toxic othering has been woven into our cultures, norms, policies, and laws all through history and then finding ways to shine light on these embedded injustices, finding ways to alter these norms laws and policies in such a way that they transition from toxic othering to normal othering. 'Normal othering' can be benign; diversity is good, natural, and productive for all human life. We need to find ways to organize social life on this planet such that only normal othering happens. When this situation exists, we have tamed the Hydra.

Ascribed status and false consciousness

Every introduction to sociology text published in the last 50 years has a section defining ascribed and achieved statuses. Ascribed statuses are typically defined as those which are given to try at birth, with examples including race, ethnicity, and gender, among others. Simple, right? But looking through the lens of critical Hydra theory the fact that 'ascribe' is a verb and infers a subject, as in 'she ascribed John's bad mood to his upset stomach.' This raises a critically important question, namely when a sociologist says a status is ascribed, who is the subject of this verb? Who says this person is 'Black' or 'white', 'male' or 'female' (etc.)? The answer is that the culture does, tradition and 'common sense' does. But in our quest to lay bare the privileging forces, all based on the ascribed status, we must entertain the idea that those in power throughout history, collectively and individually, have done the ascribing motivated by a desire to create or maintain a status quo which reinforced the toxic othering that is keeping them in a position of 'superiority.' False consciousness is buying into the assumption that one's ascribed status is permanent, immutable, and 'natural.' Rejecting false consciousness and taming the Hydra mean questioning all our ascribed statuses and rejecting the culturally embedded marginalization and normalization that come with these statuses.

Our class discussed how the Rohingya in Cox's Bazar have the ascribed status 'refugee', and how the UNHCR (United Nations High Commission on Refugees) officially certified them as such. Indeed, most of the global community accepts this act of labelling. But is embracing this devalued social status an act of false consciousness? I have no glib answer to that question, but I am certain that is a useful question to pose to myself and, more to the point, for the 'refugees' themselves to pose to themselves.

'Good trouble' and emergent norms

The concept of culture is perhaps the most important of all the social science terms. Unfortunately, many understand culture as something fixed and external to the individual, as a blueprint for living most of us follow most of the time. This model of culture is demonstratively wrong, and most sociologists and anthropologists understand culture to be organic, ever changing and adapting. As anthropologist <u>Miles Richardson</u> put it long ago culture is creativity, it is what we as humans do every day. We create culture and, as such, are able to enact social change.

One way this can happen is through changing one's behavior and creating new norms. Many emergent norms disappear quickly in a culture (think fashion trends that come and go), but those new norms which resonate with others and, I believe, which reflect fundamental human values, can catch on, spreading like a virus from one mind to another and modifying the collective behavior of masses of people.

> *"DO NOT GET LOST IN A SEA OF DESPAIR. BE HOPEFUL, BE OPTIMISTIC. OUR STRUGGLE IS NOT THE STRUGGLE OF A DAY, A WEEK, A MONTH, OR A YEAR, IT IS THE STRUGGLE OF A LIFETIME. NEVER, EVER BE AFRAID TO MAKE SOME NOISE AND GET IN GOOD TROUBLE, NECESSARY TROUBLE."*
> — *REPRESENTATIVE JOHN LEWIS*

'Be the change you want to see in the world;' can, cynically, be seen as just another vacuous phrase, but I beg to differ. The late Congressperson John Lewis urged us to cause 'good trouble', i.e., being positive deviants acting in ways that confront all forms of exploitation. In line with taming the Hydra he urged us to,

"Continue to build union between movements stretching across the globe because we must put away our willingness to profit from the exploitation of others."

Given the intersectionality of the privileging forces represented in the Hydra model 'building union between movements' indeed must be our constant goal.

Positive deviants

At first, he Rohingya and Bangladeshi learners had trouble with the phrase 'positive deviance' but through Azizul's adept translation skills most finally understood that being a leader in the community and a positive agent of social change means sticking out of the crowd, deviating from the cultural norms that marginalize others. Creating and supporting emergent norms that question embedded marginalizing forces is the job of a humanitarian leader.

Bending the moral arc toward justice and taming the Hydra depends on an infinite number of small acts on each of our parts all geared toward changing social norms, policies in our personal lives, organizations with which we work, in our communities, and in laws at the local, national, and international levels. We need to raise our voices not just as informal agents of social control and social change, but consistently urge those who are formal agents of social change, our politicians and thought leaders in organizations and businesses, to accept and fight for change. We need to urge all these individuals through our phone calls, texts, emails, and one-on-one conversations to change each and every policy and law which contributes to toxic othering. This path is difficult because some of our cultures and even our laws have demonized and marginalized some statuses. Making 'good trouble' is going to be difficult for many.

The way forward is not easy; the forces that want to bend the moral arc in a negative direction are strong, and they are represented in some of the leadership we have around the world right now. Look at what's happening in Ethiopia. Look at what is happening in Myanmar. Look at what is happening in Palestine. Look what is happening in the United States. There are many who fight this anti-toxic othering work because they personally benefit, or they are motivated by hatred and fear, driven by some base impulses, namely gluttony and greed.

Some changes will be harder than others. Hetero/cisnormativity is a problem, and the acceptance of different sexualities and gender identifications is something that flies in the face of much cultural learning for many people around the world. I understand that the hill is a very steep one for many people.

Similarly, because race, ethnicity, religion, and politics are so inextricably combined in so many cultures it will be difficult for some to accept all humans as deserving of equality and dignity. Perhaps the biggest issue regarding toxic othering is the issue related to anthropocentrism. We tend to see ourselves as, of course, dominant over nature, and this relationship is clearly one which is toxic both metaphorically and literally.

Taming the Hydra means slowly reconstructing our cultures, purging those norms and structures which perpetuate toxic othering. Change will be difficult and must be done in a measured and sober fashion, always motivated by love and compassion.

A beginning

Our team has now completed the Introduction to Sociology training course for this small group of Rohingya and Bangladeshi learners, and recently we had a 'graduation' ceremony. I will be following up with these individuals to see the lasting value of our class, but at this moment I am confident that this new team of 'Hydra tamers' will cause good trouble in the refugee camps and in their local communities. There is much to learn from each other and from applying critical Hydra theory to all the questions we raised during our months together. In my final comments to the learners, I charged them to use the conceptual tools they gained through this course -most prominently the Hydra model- to be leaders in their communities and agents of positive social change. This same charge goes to any who read this book.

Postscript

A very special guest at our certificate award ceremony was the Executive Director of the Centre for Peace and Justice at Brac University, the honorable Manzoor Hasan. He addressed the learners, congratulating them on their achievement. In his comments he observed that the way we had conducted the class reflected these words from Paulo Freire

Manzoor Hasan
Brac University

"The educator has the duty of not being neutral." Indeed, our conversations about such topics as gender-based violence and the oppression of various marginalized groups was anything but neutral.

This quotation comes from the book *We Make the Road by Walking: Conversations on Education and Social Change*, but Freire is most known for his book *Pedagogy of the Oppressed*. In that book he states,

> *"... the fact that certain members of the oppressor class join the oppressed in their struggle for liberation, thus moving from one pole of the contradiction to the other ... Theirs is a fundamental role and has been throughout the history of this struggle. It happens, however, that as they cease to be exploiters or indifferent spectators or simply the heirs of exploitation and move to the side of the exploited, they almost always bring with them the marks of their origin: their prejudices and their deformations, which include a lack of confidence in the people's ability to think, to want, and to know. Accordingly, these adherents to the people's cause constantly run the risk of falling into a type of generosity as malefic as that of the oppressors. The generosity of the oppressors is nourished by an unjust order, which must be maintained to justify that generosity. Our converts, on the other hand, truly desire to transform the unjust order; but because of their background they believe that they must be the executors of the transformation. They talk about the people, but they do not trust them; and trusting the people is the indispensable precondition for revolutionary change. A real humanist can be identified more by his trust in the people, which engages him in their struggle, than by a thousand actions in their favor without that trust."*

I was humbled to have my name uttered in the same sentence as Paolo Freire, and it gave me pause. Reflecting now about my experience I can say full throatily that I absolutely trusted my colleague Azizul from the very beginning of our relationship many months ago. Over the weeks of our class, I grew to not only trust but to be challenged by the learners in our class.

Though I do come from the 'oppressor class' I have worked hard to continually identify and address the 'marks of my origin' and now see my liberation bound up in the fight for the liberation of all humans. I do believe that a true humanist must trust those with which they partner but also must trust -and walk forward with- humanity as a whole.

Chapter 21
Applying Critical Hydra Theory on Tuesday morning

Paris, 2021

Later this fall I will take part in a panel session at the 6th meeting of the International Humanitarian Studies Association (IHSA) meeting in Paris. As co-organizer of this panel, I will have the duty of opening our session with some remarks intended to frame our discussions related to the panel's theme "Privileging Forces in the Humanitarian System: Power and Marginalization". It seems fitting that this next phase of talking about what I have called 'Critical Hydra Theory' will take place in the context of a conference since this conceptual journey had its beginning at the ALNAP meeting in Berlin in 2019.

My goal will be to introduce the Hydra model and urge those listening to embrace this conceptual tool. Though having a longer history, the commonly heard phrase, "I suppose it is tempting, if the only tool you have is a hammer, to treat everything as if it were a nail" is attributed to American psychologist Abraham Maslow. Although disparaged as cognitive bias, I will argue that in this case the tool that I will encourage people to use has broad application, especially regarding the topic for our panel. The Hydra model is all about shining a light on 'power and marginalization.'

Critical Hydra Theory

Specifically, I will be explaining 'Critical Hydra Theory' (CHT), pointing out that the phrase has its origins in 'Critical Race Theory' (CRT) but that it is more comprehensive, interrogating not just race and ethnicity but all of the privileging forces which have historically served to marginalize the majority of humans, both past and present. Like Critical Race Theory, this new perspective has a heavy emphasis on history, the phenomena of intersectionality, and how each of the privileging forces are structured into cultural systems. Using the illustration of the Hydra, I'll briefly introduce and explain each head.

Critical Hydra Theory is a powerful metaphor for engaging critically with intersectionality and reflexively with privilege; is a novel packaging of an old idea, namely that in many -perhaps most- cases those in power will seek to normalize and justify the marginalization of the 'other'.

These processes of normalization and justification serve to weave marginalization into the very fabric of each culture leading to various levels of 'false consciousness.' Both those being marginalized and those doing the marginalization may come believe the falsehood that, for example, women are inferior to men, or that 'white' people are superior to non-white people.

Critical Hydra Theory demands taking a very controversial stance, questioning how power has been misused in the formation of nearly all cultural institutions, but especially those of family, religion, politics, law, education, and the media. Embracing CHT means interrogating all cultural assumptions, norms, policies, laws, and structures which support toxic othering in any form.

I am reminded - and cautioned by - the phrase from Hermann Hesse, "The bird fights its way out of the egg. The egg is the world. Who would be born must first destroy a world." Acting on lessons learned from CHT means being sober to the fact that cultures are integrated and complex fabrics, and that pulling on one string may unravel essential parts of the whole. Worlds can be changed without wholesale destruction; indeed, most social change is slow and organic. The fact remains, though, hard questions must be asked regarding all forms of culturally entrenched marginalization, and this means questioning basic assumptions about each major social institution. The emphasis should not be on 'destroying a world' but rather a systematic, measured but at the same time radical -meaning to the root- transformation.

Basic tenets of Critical Hydra Theory

Embracing CHT means understanding it's basic tenets including

- All humans see each other in terms of our various -mostly ascribed- status.
- 'Normal othering' will tend to degenerate into 'toxic othering' whenever there is an asymmetry of power between one status group and another. 'Toxic othering' leads to the normalization of marginalization, entrenching itself deeply into cultural norms, rules, policies, laws, and religious and political dogma.
- All privileging forces are driven by 'toxic othering' and throughout history these forces have impacted the life chances of those marginalized.
- The intersectionality inherent between all the privileging forces must be recognized and addressed. Each privileging force can be seen separately, of course, but probing into how each force reinforces and amplifies the others is essential.
- Critical to CHT is understanding that 'false consciousness' exists and that there can be a cultural blindness as to the existence of various privileging forces afflicting both the group in power and those being marginalized.
- Listening to the voices of and taking the lead from those who are marginalized, and especially those who are marginalized by multiple privileging forces, is a primary tool for those using CHT. This means taking to heart the aphorism, "Until the lion learns to speak, tales of hunting will always favor the hunter" and actively listening to the 'lion.'
- The desired end goal is for 'toxic othering' to be replaced by 'normal othering' where differences are recognized, honored, and respected by all. This goal can be reached by addressing abuses of power and finding ways to emphasize the importance of using the positive forces of love and compassion to affect social change.

Tuesday morning

Humanitarian workers, especially those involved in getting aid to victims of natural or human made disasters, do critical work impacting countless lives. A typical workday is spent 'putting out the closest fire', with tasks prioritized based on the immediacy of the action(s) needed. The luxury of stepping back to look at a 'bigger picture' is exactly that, a luxury for which not many have the time or energy to invest. The few who have the good (?) fortune to attend the occasional workshop or conference sit in sessions knowing that next Tuesday morning they'll be back at their desk/cubicle/work site with a load of work to do, the conference 'take away points' already forgotten.

So, what can they do in response to learning about 'critical Hydra theory'? Here's two concrete steps you can do in ten minutes and access to a printer, the first more time consuming than the second.

1. Print a copy of the Hydra image (I'll send high resolution copies to anyone who asks in either black and white or color) and tape it to your wall, right next to your personal photos, etc. Then forget about it. Or not. Pretend you're an eager undergraduate for a moment and be inspired to look more deeply at yourself and the world around you through the lens of CHT. Look at the image and then in the mirror, taking 'a privilege inventory', asking yourself how you can be a better ally and/or accept offers of allyship from those with whom you work or interact with daily. Seek to understand power. Be unafraid to cause 'good trouble' occasionally. Be the change (there, I said it).

2. Copy and send the following email to your organization's leadership, cc'ing any others you deem relevant, i.e., in a position to affect change.

   Subject line:
   Big picture questions

   Body of email:

   I hope this email finds you well. Recently I attended a workshop [read a book] which used the metaphor of a Hydra to frame various chronic social justice issues (see attached illustration). We were introduced to "Critical Hydra Theory" (CHT) which is like Critical Race Theory on steroids, hitting on not just one privileging force but eight; it is very inclusive. Using what I understand of CHT, here are some questions about our organization that I would like to raise. These questions are neither simple nor uncontentious, but are very important, perhaps existentially so.

Answering these questions will involve many person-hours, I understand, and will thus necessitate funding. Educating our donors to the fact that such efforts ultimately do directly support our mission is leadership's job. Keep in mind that this model is very inclusive and by focusing on all eight heads there will be a natural 'economy of scale', a cost and time saving feature donors can appreciate.

Each of these questions is important, and each deserves your full measure of attention. Please note also that these questions address our internal functioning, interactions within the local communities where we function, and our outward facing interaction with those affected by the natural or conflict related events to which we respond.

- All eight privileging forces must be considered. These include the following points: patriarchy, ableism, race/ethnicity, classism/class, colonialism/ paternalism, privilege ageism, hetero/cisnormativity, and anthropocentrism. Has our organization done a history and/or memory report on race/ethnicity in response to #BLM? Has our organization done a history and/or memory report on race/ethnicity in response to #MeToo? If not, these should be initiated, if so, they should be used as a model for similar interrogations regarding all the other privileging forces? What can we learn from (or teach) our sister organizations in the humanitarian sector about how to do these kinds of reports?
- Internally, what are some examples of changes in corporate culture, norms, and policies that have addressed any of the heads? Consider making all within our organization aware of

these actions and changes to further normalize the shedding light on and then rejecting all manifestations of 'toxic othering'.

- How is our organization addressing the #decolonizeaid movement internally, regarding our host communities, and regarding the affected populations we serve?
- How 'green' are we and what efforts is our organization engaged in to lower our carbon footprint and to encourage those with which we work to do the same?
- Has our organization done its parts to work with our sister organizations to coordinate efforts addressing each of the Hydra-related issues?

Yes, I realize the questions above can seem overwhelming, but to repeat a point I made above, having answers to these questions is mission critical.

Best,
[signed]

Now what?

Those two actions completed you can now proceed with your Tuesday morning. My most sincere hope is that you spread the idea of CHT to others and virus-like it can spread, infecting them with the idea that toxic othering is a root cause of most of the social justice issues humanity faces. CHT is a conceptual tool that can be used to understand and address much that is wrong with how we treat each other, so be unafraid to see everything as a nail when you pick up this particular hammer. Let me know about your successes and the challenges you face. Together we can use CHT to create a more just world for all where diversity is respected, and structural inequities are minimized.

Appendix

Evolution of the Hydra in images

The Hydra metaphor almost demands a visual representation, and as soon as I was invited to be part of the ALNAP session I asked artist Dr. Ahmed Fadaam, my friend and colleague, to create an image for me. Over the nearly two years that I have been working on the Hydra model, Ahmed has added words and features dutifully. He is now working on a 3D model that can morph showing the Hydra being tamed and 'toxic' othering changing into 'normal' othering. The 'othering' process is something I have used for years in my sociology classes, and just as the Hydra changed over the last two years so has the graphic, I have used to present the idea of othering.

Throughout this book, you have seen the development of both images; here they are in chronological order.

See below how these ideas have morphed and deepened over the nearly two years of their existence.

The Hydra image

The Hydra image is now in its fourth version. This image was the first one created after I began preparations for the October 2019 ALNAP conference. This was the fruit of discussions with Leah Campbell and others at ALNAP about the topic of our 'jigsaw' session. Soon after we started using the phrase 'privileging forces' to describe all these 'isms.' In Berlin it was added, namely Ableism and Ageism. This version of the Hydra lasted well over a year, quickly apparent there were two more heads to be. After presenting the Hydra model to my sociology classes over several semesters, one more head needed to be added, Anthropocentrism, this to address our species toxic relationship with the environment.

The most recent change to the image came just this summer. I was explaining the concept of 'othering' to my learners in Bangladesh and realized the image needed to clearly represent the idea that toxic othering is the process underlying all the privileging forces.

Explaining 'othering'

Here is the original image that I have used for years to illustrate in symbols the basic idea of ethnocentrism. When I began seeing all the 'isms' as being related, this explanation served well.

A ≠ B

∴

A > B

A is different from B therefore A is better than B.

This second image adds the words 'differentiation' and 'stratification', concepts I feel are critical to a deeper understanding of the process.

A ≠ B   Differentiation...

∴   **almost always leads to**

A > B   Stratification.

A is different from B therefore A is better than B.

Adding the word "Othering" as a title was an overdue step.

This summer while teaching learners in Bangladesh the term 'othering' they found the distinction between 'normal' and 'toxic' othering to be useful.

Packing even more information into the graphic, a previously implied phrase was added, "The core process that generates privileging forces of the Hydra" underneath the title.

'Othering'

The core process that generates
the privileging forces of the Hydra

$A \neq B$

Group A is different from group B
Differentiation
'Normal/non-toxic othering'

$A > B$

Group A is superior to group B
Stratification
'Toxic othering'

The most recent iteration adds the critical dimension of power, a fundamental point that generates much discussion.

'Othering'

The core process that generates the privileging forces of the Hydra

$A \neq B$

Group A is different from group B
Differentiation
'Normal/non-toxic othering'

*Whenever there is an
asymmetry of power between
A and B there exists a strong possibility
that differentiation will morph
into stratification.*

$A > B$

Group A is superior to group B
Stratification
'Toxic othering'

Final thoughts

Just as with the rest of this book, I am sure that both the image of the Hydra and the graphic explaining 'othering' will continue to be improved. Constant critical feedback from my students, humanitarian friends and colleagues, and casual readers is always not only welcome but is fundamentally central to this journey.

References: For More Information:

Chapter 1 The Relevance Question

"ALNAP is looking for Your Ideas to Help Shape Our 32nd Annual Meeting." May 8, 2019.
https://www.alnap.org/news/alnap-is-looking-for-your-ideas-to-help-shape-our-32nd-annual-meeting.

S. Swithern. "Background Paper: ALNAP 32nd Annual Meeting; More Relevant? 10 Ways to Approach What People Really Need." September 30, 2019. ALNAP.
https://www.alnap.org/help-library/background-paper-alnap-32nd-annual-meeting-more-relevant-10-ways-to-approach-what.

"More Relevant? 10 Ways to Approach What People Really Need." ALNAP 32nd Annual Meeting Background Paper. 15-16 October 2019. Berlin German.
https://www.alna"p.org/system/files/content/resource/files/main/32-AM-Background-Paper-More-relevant.pdf.

Madison Lahr, F. Rivera, R. K. Powers, A. Mounier, B. Copsey, F. Crivellaro, J. E. Edung, J. M. Maillo Fermandez, C. Kiarie, J. Lawrence, A. Leakey, E, Mbua, H. Miller, A. Muigai, D. M. Mukhongo, A. Van Baelen, R. Wood, J. L. Schwennenger, R. Guin, H. Achyathan, A. Wilshaw and R. A. Foley. "Inter-group Violence Among Early Holocene Hunter-Gatherers of West Turkana, Kenya." *Nature* 20, January 2016. https://www.nature.com/articles/nature16477.

Brian Handwerk. "An Ancient Brutal Massacre May Be the Earliest Evidence of War." *Smithsonian Magazine.* January 20, 2016.
https://www.smithsonianmag.com/science-nature/ancient-brutal-massacre-may-be-earliest-evidence-war-180957884/.

Joseph H. Manson, Richard W. Wrangham, James L. Boone, Bernard Chapais, R. I. M Dudnbar, Carol R. Ember, William Irons, L. F. Marchant, W. C. McGrew, Toshisada Nishida, James D. Paterson, Eric Alden Smith, Craig B. Stanford, and Carol M. Worthman. "Intergroup Aggression in Chimpanzee and Hand Human [and Comments and Replies]. *Current Anthropology.* Vol. 12, No. 4. August 4-October 1991. PP. 369-390. https://www.jstor.org/stable/2743814?seq=1.
Edward W, Said. *Orientalism.* New York: Vintage, 1979.

John A. Powell and Stephen Menendian. "The Problem of Othering: Towards Inclusiveness and Belonging," *Other and Belonging.*
http://www.otheringandbelonging.org/the-problem-of-othering/.

S. R. Moosavinia, N. Niazi Ahmad Ghaforian. "Edward Said's *Orientalism* and the Study of the Self and the Other in Orwell's Burmese Days." *Studies in Literature and Language.* Research Gate 2011.
https://www.researchgate.net/publication/50934015_Edward_Said%27s_Orientali sm_and_the_Study_of_the_Self_and_the_Other_in_Orwell%27s_Burmese_Days.

Paul Buhle. *No Laughing Matter: An Analysis of Sexual Humor*. Review. Duke University Press. No. 25. Fall 1985. PP. 133-135.
https://muse.jhu.edu/article/428565/pdf.

"Universal Declaration of Human Rights." United Nations. General Assembly Resolution 217-A. December 10, 1948. https://www.un.org/en/universal-declaration-human-rights/.

Martin Luther King. "Dr. Martin Luther King, Jr. We Shall Overcome." Uploaded by Evan Woodson. 1/20/2014.
https://www.youtube.com/watch?v=VeHNbGE3tJw.

"Kimberlé Crenshaw on Intersectionality, more than Two Decades Later." *Columbia Law School.* June 8, 2017.
https://www.law.columbia.edu/news/archive/kimberle-crenshaw-intersectionality-more-two-decades-later.

Chapter 2 – Privileging Forces

ALNAP. https://www.alnap.org/.

Civilizations and Its Discontents." Wikipedia.
https://en.wikipedia.org/wiki/Civilization_and_Its_Discontents.

"The Sane Society." Wikipedia.
https://en.wikiquote.org/wiki/The_Sane_Society.

Chapter 3 – Humanitarian Principles and Intersectionality

Kimberlé Crenshaw. "Demarginalizing the Intersection of Race and Sex: Black Feminist Critique of Antidiscrimination Doctrine, Feminist Theory and Antiracist Politics." University of Chicago Legal Forum. Vol 1989, Issue 1, Article 8. https://chicagounbound.uchicago.edu/cgi/viewcontent.cgi?article=1052&context=uclf.

Tom Arcaro. "White Savior Complex." Blog. March 30, 2019. https://blogs.elon.edu/aidworkervoices/?p=1309.

"The Grand Bargain." IASC. https://interagencystandingcommittee.org/grand-bargain.

Chapter 4 – The Gaping Hole in the Hydra Model: Religious Persecution

Shoon Naing, Thu Thu Aung. "Suu Kyi to Contest Rohingya Genocide Case at World Court." *Reuters*. 11/20/2019. https://www.reuters.com/article/us-myanmar-rohingya/suu-kyi-to-contest-rohingya-genocide-case-at-world-court-idUSKBN1XU1WR.

"Bangladesh/Myanmar: Situation in the People's Republic of Bangladesh/Republic of the Union of Myanmar." Cour Pénale Internationale. 1CC-01/19. https://www.icc-cpi.int/bangladesh-myanmar.

Angelina E. Theodorou. "Which Countries Still Outlaw Apostasy and Blasphemy?" Factbank. *Pew Research Center*. July 24, 2016. https://www.pewresearch.org/fact-tank/2016/07/29/which-countries-still-outlaw-apostasy-and-blasphemy/.

Bilal Kuchay. "In India's Democracy, Muslims Feel Increasingly Marginalized." *Al Ja Jazeera*. April 23, 2019. https://www.aljazeera.com/news/2019/04/24/in-indias-democracy-muslims-feel-increasingly-marginalised/.

Grame Wood. "What ISIS Really Wants?" *The Atlantic*. March 2015. https://www.theatlantic.com/magazine/archive/2015/03/what-isis-really-wants/384980/.

Mohammed Daraghmen. "Palestinians Protest US Settlement Decision in 'Day of Rage'." *AP*. 11/26/2019. https://apnews.com/article/f2049665002045869da66b237c3673c1.

"Anti-Muslim Activities in the United States 2012-2018." *New America*. ND. https://www.newamerica.org/in-depth/anti-muslim-activity/.

"Meet Three People Targeted for Being 'Atheists,' and a Muslim Leader Condemning Their Beliefs." *BBC News*. September 23, 2016. https://www.bbc.com/news/blogs-trending-34338691.

Lindsay Maizland. "China's Repression of Uighurs in Xinjiang." *Council on Foreign Relations*. 6/30/2020. https://www.cfr.org/backgrounder/chinas-repression-uighurs-xinjiang.

"Myanmar Military Leaders Must Face Genocide Charges – UN Report." *UN News*. 27/8/2018. https://news.un.org/en/story/2018/08/1017802.

"A Closer Look at How Religious Restrictions Have Risen Around the World." *Pew Research Center*, July 15, 2019.

LilTeK2. "Prevailing World Religions Map." Wikipedia. https://en.wikipedia.org/wiki/Major_religious_groups#/media/File:Prevailing_wor ld_religions_map.png.

"Since 2007, Increasing Number of Countries Have High Levels of Government Restrictions on Religion, Social Hostilities Involving Religion." Pew Research Center. July 13, 2019. https://www.pewforum.org/2019/07/15/a-closer-look-at-how-religious-restrictions-have-risen-around-the-world/pf_07-15-19_religiousrestrictions-0-01/.

Kyaw Kyaw Rebel Riot. *Fuck Religious Rules and War.* YouTube. April 2, 2013. Video. https://www.youtube.com/watch?v=GExcEfO7vB8/

World Vision. https://www.worldvision.org/.

Chapter 5 – The Ultimate Goal of the Hydra Is Genocide

Max Colchester. "Britain Gears Up for the Most Divisive Election in Decades." *Wall Street Journal*. December 8, 2019. https://www.wsj.com/articles/britain-gears-up-for-its-most-divisive-election-in-decades-11575814301.

"Stories About Impeachment." NPR. No Date.
https://www.npr.org/tags/216163255/impeachment.

"Republic of the Gambia v. Republic of the Union of Myanmar: Application Instituting Proceedings and Request for Provisional Measures." International Court of Justice. November 2019. https://www.icj-cij.org/files/case-related/178/178-20191111-APP-01-00-EN.pdf.

"Multimedia Galleries. International Court of Justice. Website. https://www.icj-cij.org/en/multimedia-index.

Tom Arcaro. "Mobile and Wi-Fi Access a Basic Human right? Yes!" *Aid Workers Voices*. Blog. November 15, 2019.
https://blogs.elon.edu/aidworkervoices/?p=1538

Yeu Ninje. International Court of Justice. en.wikipedia. Public domain.

The Sane Society. New York: Open Road Integrated Media. 1955.
"III. Discrimination in Arakan." Human Rights Watch. ND.
https://www.hrw.org/reports/2000/burma/burm005-02.htm.

Tom Arcaro and Zayed Jack. "The Story of Esoup: A Victim of Persecution." *Rohingya Post*. 4/12/2016.
https://www.rohingyapost.com/the-story-of-esoup-a-victim-of-persecution/.

"Independent International Fact-Finding Mission on Myanmar." United National Human Rights Council. March 2017.
https://www.ohchr.org/en/hrbodies/hrc/myanmarffm/pages/index.aspx.

Chapter 6 – ALNAP Comments, Berlin 2019

32nd Annual Meeting Program." 2019 ALNAP Meeting, October 15-16, 2019. Berlin, Germany.
https://www.alnap.org/system/files/content/resource/files/main/alnap-32-am-programme.pdf.

Arbie Baguios. "How Can Aid Be RE-imaged for a New World?" Aid-Reimaged. Linked in, October 8, 2019.
https://www.linkedin.com/pulse/how-can-aid-re-imagined-new-world-arbie-baguios?articleId=6587278331853455361#comments-6587278331853455361&trk=public_profile_article_view.

Thomas Arcaro. *Understanding the Global Experiences: Becoming a Responsible World Citizen.* 2009.

Chapter 7 – Yet Another Head on the Hydra

ALNAP. "ALNAP 32nd Annual Meeting.' October 15-16, 2019. Hosted by the German Federal Foreign Office. Berlin, Germany.
https://www.alnap.org/upcoming-events/annual-meetings/alnap-32nd-annual-meeting.

Tom Arcaro's series of blogs based on the ALNAP Experience. "Hydra 'Privileging Forces'." Series of blogs inspired by ALNAP and Hydra. Written from November 2, 2019, until September 25, 2020.
https://blogs.elon.edu/aidworkervoices/?cat=396404.

Whiskey Tango Foxtrot. Craig Zobel, director. 2016. 112 minutes.
https://www.imdb.com/title/tt3553442/.

"Wet Hooch" clip. *Whiskey Tango Foxtrot.* 2016.
https://www.youtube.com/watch?v=MLJnbke6HUY.

Anne Haas and Stanford W. Gregory, Jr. "The Impact of Physical Attractiveness on Women's Social Status and International Power."
https://www.jstor.org/stable/4540908?seq=1#metadata_info_tab_contents.

Rachel A. Gordon, Robert Crosnee, and Wue Wang. "Physical Attractiveness and the Accumulation of Social and Human Capital in Adolescence and Young Adulthood Assets and Distractions."
https://www.ncbi.nlm.nih.gov/pmc/articles/PMC5558203/.

Deborah Rhode. *The Beauty of Bias: The Injustice of Appearance in Life and Law.* New York: Oxford University Press. 2010.

Viren Swami and Natalie Salem. "The Evolutionary Psychology of Human Beauty."
https://www.researchgate.net/publication/282855653_The_evolutionary_psychology_of_human_beauty.

"Global Cosmetic Predicts Market Will Reach USD 863 Billion by 2024: Zion Market Research." Zion Market Report. June 22, 2018. https://www.globenewswire.com/news-release/2018/06/22/1528369/0/en/Global-Cosmetic-Products-Market-Will-Reach-USD-863-Billion-by-2024-Zion-Market-Research.html.

"Global Humanitarian Assistance Report 2019."
Development Initiatives. Global Humanitarian Assistance. 2019. https://reliefweb.int/sites/reliefweb.int/files/resources/GHA%20report%202019_0.pdf.

Chapter 8 – A Code of Ethics for Privileged Anti-Othering Persons: The Humanitarian Imperative and Hydra Revisited

"In the Eyes of Others: How People in Crisis Perceive Humanitarian Aid." 19 December 2011. Médecins Sans Frontières. https://www.msf.org/eyes-others-how-people-crises-perceive-humanitarian-aid.

Matthew Teague. "Abiding by the Confederate Flag Ban Inside Talladega, Grudgingly. *The New York Times.* June 21, 2020, updated June 26, 2020. https://www.nytimes.com/2020/06/21/sports/autoracing/talladega-nascar-confederate-flag.html.

Brittany Shammas. "Mississippi Lawmakers Pass Resolution Paving Way to Remove Confederate Symbol from State Flag." *The Washington Post.* June 27, 2020. https://www.washingtonpost.com/nation/2020/06/27/mississippi-flag-vote/.

"MSF Updates on Racism. Mèdicins San Frontières. 10 August 2020. https://www.doctorswithoutborders.ca/article/msf-updates-racism.

Ben Parker. Mèdecins San Frontières Needs 'Radical Change' on Racism: MSF President." *The New Humanitarian.* 24 June 2020. https://www.thenewhumanitarian.org/news/2020/06/24/MSF-racism-black-lives-matter-debate.

Yves Daccord. "The Humanitarian #MeToo Crisis: The Really Hard Work Is Just Beginning." Relief Web. 19 November 2018. https://www.thenewhumanitarian.org/news/2020/06/24/MSF-racism-black-lives-matter-debate.

"ALNAP 32nd Annual Meeting." 15-16 October 2019. ALNAP. https://www.alnap.org/upcoming-events/annual-meetings/alnap-32nd-annual-meeting.

"Hydra" (artwork). Concept by Thomas Arcaro. Artwork by Ahmed al-Fadaam. Elon University.

Powell, John A. "US vs. Them: the sinister techniques of "Othering' – and how to avoid them. *The Guardian.* 8 November 2017. https://www.theguardian.com/inequality/2017/nov/08/us-vs-them-the-sinister-techniques-of-othering-and-how-to-avoid-them.

Tim Wise. "Code of Ethics for Anti-Racists." *Medium Race.* June 16. https://medium.com/@timjwise/code-of-ethics-for-white-anti-racists-103914639dd7.

Tom Arcaro. "White Savior Complex." Aid Worker's Voices. March 30, 2019. https://blogs.elon.edu/aidworkervoices/?p=1309

Kimberlé Crenshaw on Intersectionality, More than Two Decades Later." *Columbia Law School.* June 8, 2017. https://www.law.columbia.edu/news/archive/kimberle-crenshaw-intersectionality-more-two-decades-later.

"Universal Declaration of Human Rights." United Nations. https://www.un.org/en/universal-declaration-human-rights/.

"Putting the Power of Law in People's Hands." NAMATI Organization. https://namati.org/.

Martin Luther King. "I Have a Dream." NPR. January.20, 2020. https://www.npr.org/2010/01/18/122701268/i-have-a-dream-speech-in-its-entirety

John Lewis. "Together, You Can Redeem the South of Our Nation." (Posthumous opinion piece). *The New York Times.* July 30, 2020. https://www.nytimes.com/2020/07/30/opinion/john-lewis-civil-rights-america.html.

John Lewis. House of Representatives. https://commons.wikimedia.org/wiki/File:John_Lewis-2006_(cropped).jpg.

John Lewis: Good Trouble. Magnolia Pictures and Magnet Releasing. May 11, 2020. https://www.youtube.com/watch?v=z_oEkOdIXdo.

"bell hooks." ND. Berea College. Loyal Jones Appalachian Center. https://www.berea.edu/appalachian-center/appalachian-center-home/faculty-and-staff/bell-hooks/.

"Feminist Model." ND. 4202: Models of Conflict Resolution. https://sites.google.com/a/pdx.edu/models-of-conflict-resolution/home/feminist-model.

Pangambam S. 2016." Full Transcript: President Kennedy's Peace Speech at American University (June 10, 1963). *The Singju Post.* May 16. https://singjupost.com/full-transcript-president-kennedys-peace-speech-at-american-university-june-10-1963/.

"The 1619 Project Curriculum." ND. Pulitzer Center. https://pulitzercenter.org/lesson-plan-grouping/1619-project-curriculum. "Global Climate Change." NASA. https://climate.nasa.gov/.

"The Better Angels of Our Nature" ND *Wikipedia.* https://en.wikipedia.org/wiki/The_Better_Angels_of_Our_Nature.

Steven Pinker. 2011. *The Better Angels of Our Nature: Why Violence Has Declined.* New York: Viking Press.

"The Great Dictator." ND. *Wikipedia.* https://en.wikipedia.org/wiki/The_Great_Dictator.

Chaplin, Charlie. 1949. *The Great Dictator.* Director, Producer and Author. Los Angeles: United Artists.

Charlie Chaplin. 2016. "Charlie Chaplin: Final Speech from *The Great Dictator." YouTube.* https://www.youtube.com/watch?v=J7GY1Xg6X20.

Bending the Arc. 2017. Matt Damon, Ben Affleck and Geralyn Drayfour, Executive Producers. Impact Partners. https://bendingthearcfilm.com/.

Chapter 9 – More on the Origin of the Hydra Concept

"ALNAP: 32nd Annual Meeting Announcement." No date. ALNAP. https://www.alnap.org/upcoming-events/annual-meetings/alnap-32nd-annual-meeting.

Stuart Schussler. "The Zapatistas and the Capitalist Hydra: Theorizing and Responding to Mexico's Crisis." No date. Academic Org.

Tom Arcaro. "PWP." You Tube. December 5, 2018. https://www.youtube.com/watch?v=JDahactSSOM.

Chiapas Support Committee. "EZLN: We Will Go to Find What Makes Us Equal//Despite Oblivion We Live." Compañero Manual Blog on Zapatistas and Mexico. October 7, 2020. https://chiapas-support.org/2020/10/07/ezln-we-will-go-to-find-what-makes-us-equal-despite-oblivion-we-live/?fbclid=IwAR03eXL26eEe2jGrJjUf9CC0nHC4U96aJPN3fSIWGSRq5V_o808ORm8XEK0.

Chapter 10 – The Hydra Just Grew Another Head

Tom Arcaro. "A Code of Ethics for Privileged and Anti-Othering Persons: The Humanitarian Imperative and Hydra Revisited. Blog posted 6/29/2020. https://blogs.elon.edu/aidworkervoices/?p=1653.

Matasha Lennard. "Ecocide Should be Recognized as a Crime Against Humanity but We Can't Wait for The Hague to Judge. *The Intercept.* September 24, 2019. https://theintercept.com/2019/09/24/climate-justice-ecocide-humanity-crime/.

Ronald Waldman. "Natural and Human-Made Disasters." CDC. December 13, 2018. https://www.cdc.gov/eis/field-epi-manual/chapters/Natural-Human-Disasters.html.

"Based on Science: Global Warming Is Contributing to Extreme Weather Events." *National Academies of Sciences Engineering Medicine.* August 5, 2019. https://www.nationalacademies.org/based-on-science/climate-change-global-warming-is-contributing-to-extreme-weather-events.

"Cyclone Idai and Kenneth." UNICEF.
https://www.unicef.org/mozambique/en/cyclone-idai-and-kenneth.

"Mozambique: UN Responds as Thousands Are Caught in the Wake of Devastating Cyclone Eloise." *UN News.* January 26, 2021. https://news.un.org/en/story/2021/01/1082972.

Papa Seck. "Links Between Natural Disasters, Humanitarian Assistance and Disaster Risk Reduction: A Critical Perspective." *Humanitarian Development Report 2007/2008.* UNDP. ND.
http://hdr.undp.org/sites/default/files/seck_papa.pdf.

Crabtree, Vexen. "Sura 6 of the *Qur'an.*" The Human Truth Foundation. 2013. http://www.holybooks.info/sura_6.html.

Tom Arcaro. "Mentality of Exploitation." SOC 372. Spring 2021. https://docs.google.com/document/d/1esff9lgWMAOpShcUv6WH4rwi3G-RxifWdb9ZzbPEnLQ/edit.

Chapter 12 – Hydra Theory 101

"Works of Miguel de Unamuno." ND. *Spanish Books.*
https://www.classicspanishbooks.com/20th-cent-unamuno-works.html.

Tom Arcaro. ND. "Hydra 'Privileging Forces'." ND. Elon University.
https://blogs.elon.edu/aidworkervoices/?cat=396404.

"More Than Meets the Eye: Let's Fight Racism!" ND. United Nations. https://www.un.org/en/letsfightracism/.

Frank W. Ewell. ND. "Robert Carneiro on the Rise of the State." *Sociocultural Systems.*
http://www.faculty.rsu.edu/users/f/felwell/www/Theorists/Essays/Carneiro1.html.

Admin. "A Map of Gender-Diverse Cultures.' 2015. *Independent Lens. PBS.* August 11.
https://www.pbs.org/independentlens/content/two-spirits_map-html/.

Daniel A. Guthrie. 1971. "Primitive Man's Relationship to Nature." *Bioscience.* Vol. 21, No. 13 (July). 721-723. Oxford Press. https://www.jstor.org/stable/1295922?seq=1.

"#1 Jeff Bezos." ND. *Forbes.*
https://www.forbes.com/profile/jeff-bezos/?sh=1b4f185b1b23.

Stephen Metcalf. 2017. "New Liberalism: The Idea That Swallowed the World." *The Guardian.* August 18.
https://www.theguardian.com/news/2017/aug/18/neoliberalism-the-idea-that-changed-the-world.

Camille Bruneau. 2018. "How do Patriarchy Capitalism Jointly Reinforce the Oppression of Women?" *CADTM.* September 13.
https://www.cadtm.org/How-do-patriarchy-and-capitalism-jointly-reinforce-the-oppression-of-women.

"Capitalism and Racism: Conjoined Twins." 2019. *NFG (Neighborhood Funders Group.* September 3.
https://www.nfg.org/news/capitalism-and-racism-conjoined-twins.

Robert B. Baird. 2021. "The Innovation of Whiteness: The Long History of a Dangerous Idea." *The Guardian.* April 20.
https://www.theguardian.com/news/2021/apr/20/the-invention-of-whiteness-long-history-dangerous-idea.

William Easterly. 2015. *The Tyranny of Experts.* United Kingdom: Institute of Economic Affairs.

Tatiana Cozzarelli. 2019. "Queer Oppression Is Etched in the Heart of Capitalism.' *Left Voice.* July 5.
https://www.leftvoice.org/queer-oppression-is-etched-in-the-heart-of-capitalism.

Theodosius Dobzhansky. 1973. "Nothing in Biology Makes Sense Except in the Light of Evolution." *The American Biology Teacher.* Volume 15, Issue 3 (March).
https://online.ucpress.edu/abt/article/35/3/125/9833/Nothing-in-Biology-Makes-Sense-except-in-the-Light.

Editors. 2020. "Disability, Covid and Capitalism." MRonline. November 28.
https://mronline.org/2020/10/26/disability-covid-and-capitalism/.

Ellen Knickmeyer, Christina Larson, and Seth Borenstein. 2021. "Go Forth and Spend: Call for Action Closes US Climate Summit. *AP News.* April 23.
https://apnews.com/article/joe-biden-technology-bill-gates-climate-climate-change-5fa46b576accea6da026d8e31b8117e0.

Derald Wing Sue and Lisa Spanierman. 2020. *Microaggressions in Everyday Life*. 2nd Edition, New York: Wiley.

Chapter 14 -- The Hydra in Film References

"On the Basis of Sex"

"Patriarchy." *Merriam-Webster.com Dictionary*, Merriam-Webster. https://www.merriam-webster.com/dictionary/patriarchy. Accessed 16 Jun. 2021.

Thulin, Lila. "The True Story of the Case Ruth Bader Ginsburg Argues in 'On the Basis of Sex.'" Smithsonian Magazine, 24 December 2018. https://www.smithsonianmag.com/history/true-story-case-center-basis-sex-180971110/. Accessed 17 June 2021.

US Court of Appeals for the Tenth Circuit – 469 F.2d 466 (10th Cir. 1972). *Moritz v Commissioner. Justia US Law. https://law.justia.com/cases/federal/appellate-courts/F2/469/466/79852/.* Accessed 17 Jun. 2021.

"Race/Ethnicity"

"Humanitarian." Merriam-Webster.com Dictionary, Merriam-Webster. https://www.merriam-webster.com/dictionary/humanitarian. Accessed 17 Jun. 2021.

"Colonialism/Paternalism in *Victoria and Abdul*"

"Colonialism Noun – Definition, Pictures, Pronunciation and Usage Notes: Oxford Advanced American Dictionary at: OxfordLearnersDictionaries.com."

Colonialism Noun – Definition, Pictures, Pronunciation and Usage Notes Oxford Advanced American Dictionary at: OxfordLearnersDictionaries.com, 2021, http://www.oxfordlearnersdictionaries.com/us/definition/american_english/colonialism.

"Paternalism." *Merriam-Webster.com Dictionary*, Merriam-Webster. https://www.merriam-webster.com/dictionary/paternalism. Accessed 17 Jun. 2021.

“What Countries Were in the British Empire?” *Schoolshistory.org.uk*, Schoolshistory.org.uk, 2021, http://schoolshistory.org.uk/topics/british-empire/questions-about-the-british-empire/what-countries-were-in-the-british-empire/.

“Hetero/Cisnormativity & *My Beautiful Laundrette*”

Ebert, Roger. “My Beautiful Laundrette Movie Review (1986): Roger Ebert.” *Movie Review (1986) | Roger Ebert*, Tim Bevan, 11 Apr. 1986, www.rogerebert.com/reviews/my-beautiful-laundrette-1986.

“Joker and Classism”

“‘Joker’ and the Crisis of Capitalism.” *New Politics*, 24 Nov. 2019, https://newpol.org/joker-and-the-crisis-of-capitalism/.

Robinson, Chauncey K. “‘Joker’ Exposes the Broken Class System That Creates Its Own Monsters.” *People's World*, 4 Oct. 2019, https://peoplesworld.org/article/joker-exposes-the-broken-class-system-that-creates-its-own-monsters/.

Sociology: Understanding and Changing the Social World, 6.1, 13.2

“Ableism”

Smith, Leah. “Center for Disability Rights Inc.” *#Ableism – Center for Disability Rights*, www.cdrnys.org/blog/uncategorized/ableism/.

Woodburn, Danny, and Kristina Kopić. “ON EMPLOYMENT OF ACTORS WITH DISABILITIES IN TELEVISION.” *THE RUDERMAN WHITE PAPER*, Ruderman Family Foundation, July 2016.

Sociology: Understanding and Changing the Social World, 4.1

Lopez, Kristen. “‘Forrest Gump’ at 25: Disability Representation (For Better and Worse).” *Forbes*, Forbes Magazine, 5 July 2019, www.forbes.com/sites/kristenlopez/2019/07/05/forrest-gump-at-25-disability-representation-for-better-and-worse/?sh=81a3b00664d5.

“Ageism and *Up*”

Sociology: Understanding and Changing the Social World, 12.1, 12.3

Smith, Dr. Stacy L., Pieper, Dr. Katherine, and Marc Choueiti. "USC Annenberg Film Study: Pop Culture Stereotypes Aging Americans." Edited by Dr. Stacey L. Smith, *USC Annenberg School for Communication and Journalism*, 12 Sept. 2016, http://annenberg.usc.edu/news/faculty-research/usc-annenberg-film-study-pop-culture-stereotypes-aging-americans.

Walker, Kim. "New Disney Movie Sparks Ageism Debate." *Silver Group*, 29 Apr. 2009, http://www.silvergroup.asia/2009/04/29/new-disney-movie-sparks-ageism-debate/#:~:text=New%20Disney%20movie%20sparks%20ageism%20debate%20Apr%2029%2C,grumpy%20old%20man%2C%20is%20not%20considered%20commercially%20attractive.

Chapter 18

Arfina Osman, F., 2010. Bangladesh Politics: Confrontation, Monopoly and Crisis in Governance. Asian Journal of Political Science, [online] 18(3), pp.310-333. Available at: https://www.tandfonline.com/doi/abs/10.1080/02185377.2010.527224>

CFR, 2020. India's Muslims: An Increasingly Marginalized Population. [online] Council on Foreign Relations. Available at: https://www.cfr.org/backgrounder/india-muslims-marginalized-population-bjp-modi [Accessed 7 August 2021].

Christopher, A. (1988). 'Divide and Rule': The Impress of British Separation Policies. Area, 20(3), 233-240. Retrieved August 7, 2021, from: http://www.jstor.org/stable/20002624.

Fukuyama, F., 2018. Identity: The Demand for Dignity and the Politics of Resentment, New York, Farrar, Straus, and Giroux, 2018, 240 pp. 1st ed. New York: Farrar, Straus, and Giroux.

Hoque, M. (2016). Tea Politics and Clientelism. [Online]. Dhaka: The Daily Independent. Retrieved 14 August 2021, from: https://www.theindependentbd.com/magazine/details/45983/Tea-politics-and-clientelism.

Islam, M., 2013. The Toxic Politics of Bangladesh: A Bipolar Competitive Neopatrimonial State? Asian Journal of Political Science, 21(2), pp.148-168.

Katju, M., 2013. The truth about Pakistan. The Nation, [online] Available at: <https://web.archive.org/web/20131110103720/http://www.nation.com.pk/pakistan-news-newspaper-daily-english-online/columns/02-Mar-2013/the-truth-about-pakistan> [Accessed 7 August 2021].

Olney, J. and Hoque, M., 2021. Perceptions of Rohingya Refugees: Marriage and Social Justice After Cross-Border Displacement. [online] San Francisco: The Asia Foundation & Centre for Peace and Justice, p. 12.

Reuters, 2018. Why Facebook is losing the war on hate speech in Myanmar. [online] Reuters. Available at: <https://www.reuters.com/investigates/special-report/myanmar-facebook-hate/> [Accessed 7 August 2021].

Taylor, R., 2005. Do States Make Nations? South East Asia Research, 13(3), pp.261-286.

Tharoor, S., 2017. The Partition: The British game of 'divide and rule'. Al Jazeera, [online]. Available at: https://www.aljazeera.com/opinions/2017/8/10/the-partition-the-british-game-of-divide-and-rule [Accessed 8 August 2021].

UNDP & Search for Common Ground, 2015. SOCIAL COHESION FRAMEWORK social cohesion for stronger communities. [online] Yangon: UNDP, p.18. Available at: <https://www.sfcg.org/wp-content/uploads/2017/02/SC2-Pariticipant-Guide_English.pdf> [Accessed 7 August 2021].

Young, I., 1990. Justice and the Politics of Difference. 1st ed. PRINCETON; OXFORD: Princeton University Press.

www.ingramcontent.com/pod-product-compliance
Lightning Source LLC
Chambersburg PA
CBHW070947250726
48663CB00002B/117